W9-DDS-567

THE ROUTLEDGE ATLAS OF CLASSICAL HISTORY

OTHER ATLASES IN THIS SERIES

THE ROUTLEDGE ATLAS OF
CLASSICAL HISTORY

Fifth edition

Michael Grant

London

First published as *The Dent Atlas of Classical History* 1971 by J M Dent

Fifth edition published 1994 by Routledge
11 New Fetter Lane, London EC4P 4EE

© 1971, 1974, 1986, 1989, 1994 Michael Grant Publications Ltd

Printed and bound in Great Britain by
Butler & Tanner Ltd, Frome and London

All rights reserved. No part of this publication may be reprinted or
reproduced or utilized in any form or by any electronic, mechanical or
other means, now known or hereafter invented, including photocopying
and recording, or in any information storage or retrieval system, without
permission in writing from the publishers.

British Library Cataloguing in Publication Data
A catalogue record for this book is available from the British Library.

ISBN 0–415–11934–0 (hbk)
ISBN 0–415–11935–9 (pbk)

Preface

This is an atlas of the classical world – the ancient Greek and Roman world, which needs to be understood if we are to understand the world of today. To say that such an atlas could ever be a substitute for a historical survey would be an exaggeration. Nevertheless, geography is such a vital, indeed predominant, factor in ancient history – and such a difficult factor because of all the changes of names[1] – that the whole course of events often seems to mean practically nothing without maps, and without a lot of them, carefully devised.

Older classical atlases, apart from a varying degree of emphasis on physical aspects, tended to concentrate on political themes, and it is true enough that these stand in great need of maps. But the present volume attempts to cast the net wider, and to introduce economic, cultural, religious and other topics as well. There are also a number of town plans.

Modern research in archaeology and other fields has shown that the classical world cannot be grasped without some appreciation of what went before it. I have consequently started this book with a number of maps illustrating the Mediterranean world during the second millennium BC, and particularly during the period from 1700 BC onwards, when the international scene had already assumed a well-defined and complex appearance; and the story is carried onwards to offer brief illustrations of the Old Testament. At the other end of the story, the traditional terminal date of the ancient world, the year AD 476 when the last western emperor ceased to reign, is again not a very meaningful landmark, so I have carried on the tale until the reign of Justinian in the following century.

It will clear enough what a very great deal is owed to the talent of Arthur Banks for transcribing the written and spoken world into cartographic form. I am also most grateful to Julian Shuckburgh and Benjamin Buchan for all the assistance they rendered on behalf of the publishers, and I want to thank Jane Dorner for assistance with the index and C. R. B. Elliott for help with an earlier revised edition. Finally, I have to acknowledge a substantial debt to existing classical atlases, German and English. And I must single out, for a special word of gratitude, the *Atlas of the Classical World* edited by A. A. M. van der Heyden and H. H. Scullard for Messrs Nelson, and *Westermanns Grosser Atlas zur Weltgechichte* (Westermann, Braunschweig). N. G. L. Hammond's *Atlas of the Greek and Roman World in Antiquity* (Noyes Press, Park Ridge) is now fundamental; so is Routledge's new classical atlas.

For this fifth edition I have added new maps on the changing frontier of the Roman Empire (maps 72 and 73), on the persecution of the Christians (map 86) and on the Roman Empire in its final years (maps 88 and 90).

1994   MICHAEL GRANT

[1] Modern names are given after the ancient in the Index.

List of Maps

1

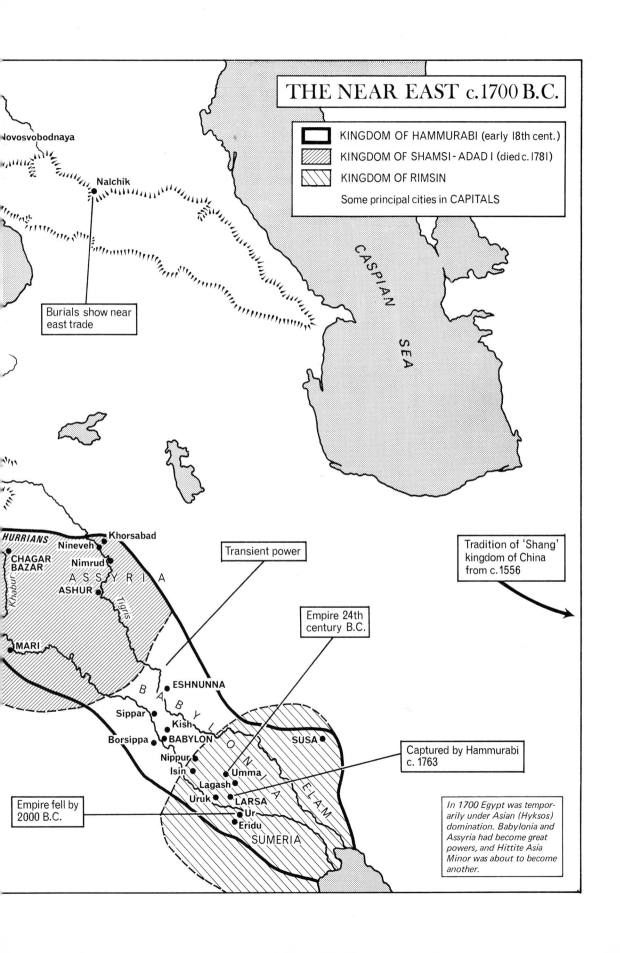

THE NEAR EAST c.1700 B.C.

☐	KINGDOM OF HAMMURABI (early 18th cent.)
▨	KINGDOM OF SHAMSI - ADAD I (died c.1781)
▨	KINGDOM OF RIMSIN
	Some principal cities in CAPITALS

Novosvobodnaya

Nalchik

CASPIAN SEA

Burials show near east trade

HURRIANS
Khorsabad
Nineveh
CHAGAR BAZAR
Nimrud
ASSYRIA
ASHUR

Khabur

Tigris

MARI

Transient power

Tradition of 'Shang' kingdom of China from c.1556

Empire 24th century B.C.

BABYLONIA

ESHNUNNA

Sippar
Kish
Borsippa
BABYLON
Nippur
Isin
Umma
Lagash
Uruk
LARSA
Ur
Eridu

SUSA

ELAM

Captured by Hammurabi c. 1763

Empire fell by 2000 B.C.

SUMERIA

In 1700 Egypt was temporarily under Asian (Hyksos) domination. Babylonia and Assyria had become great powers, and Hittite Asia Minor was about to become another.

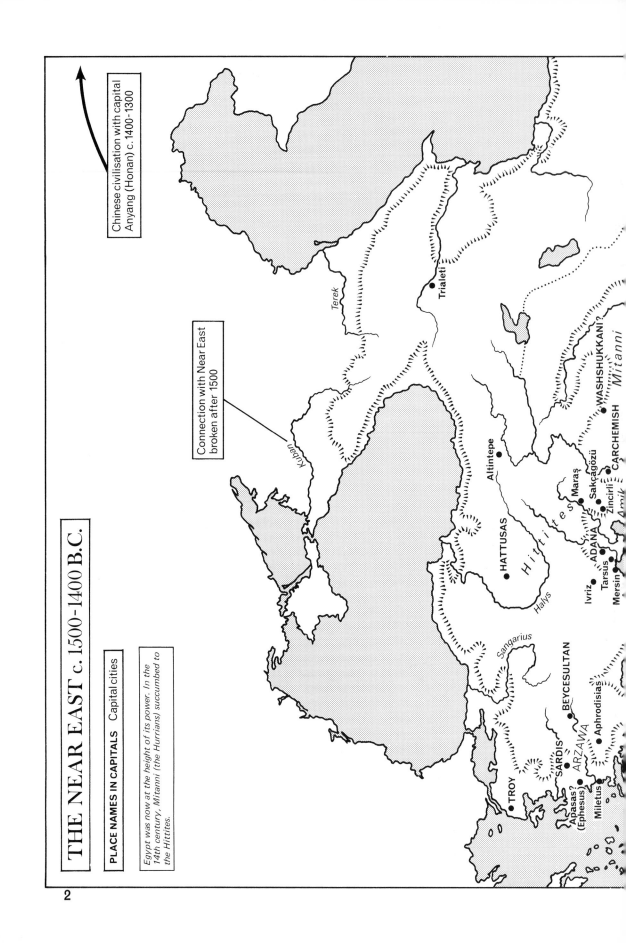

THE NEAR EAST c. 1500-1400 B.C.

PLACE NAMES IN CAPITALS Capital cities

Egypt was now at the height of its power. In the 14th century, Mitanni (the Hurrians) succumbed to the Hittites.

Chinese civilisation with capital Anyang (Honan) c. 1400-1300

Connection with Near East broken after 1500

Terek

Kuban

Trialeti

Altintepe

HATTUSAS

H i t t i t e s

Halys

Sangarius

Maraş

Sakçagözü

Zincirli

ADANA

Tarsus

Ivriz

Mersin

Amik

CARCHEMISH

WASHSHUKKANI?

Mitanni

BEYCESULTAN

SARDIS

ARZAWA

Aphrodisias

TROY

Apasas?

(Ephesus)

Miletus

2

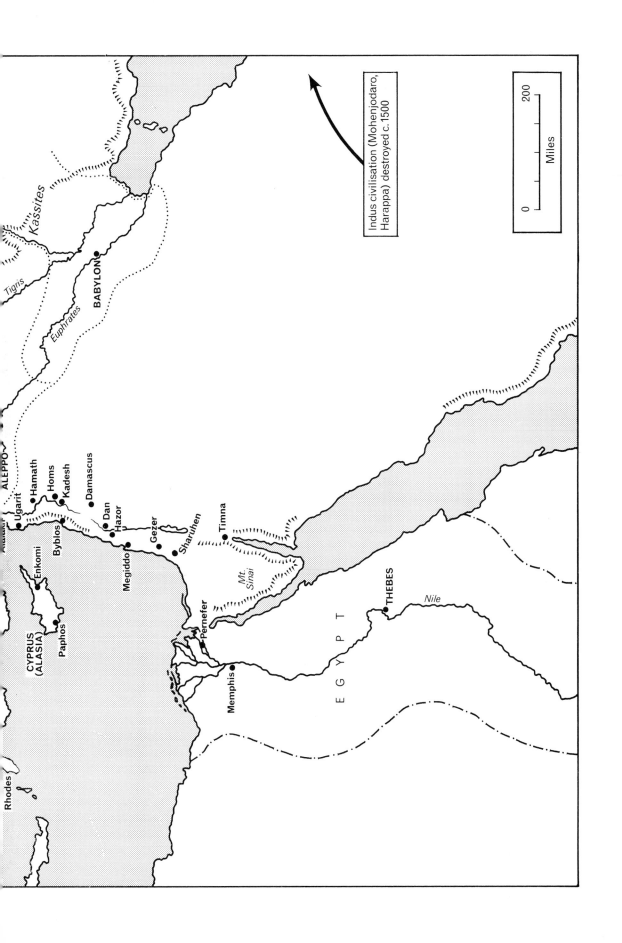

Indus civilisation (Mohenjodaro, Harappa) destroyed c. 1500

0   200
Miles

BABYLON

Tigris

Euphrates

Kassites

ALEPPO

Ugarit
Hamath
Homs
Kadesh
Damascus

Dan
Hazor
Gezer
Sharuhen
Timna

Byblos

Megiddo

Mt. Sinai

Enkomi

CYPRUS
(ALASIA)

Paphos

Rhodes

Pernefer

Memphis

THEBES

Nile

E G Y P T

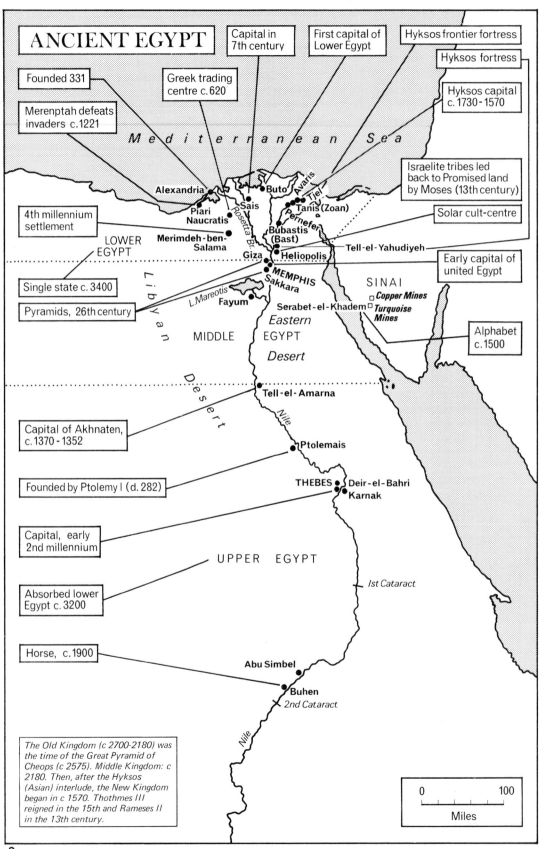

ANCIENT EGYPT

Capital in 7th century

First capital of Lower Egypt

Hyksos frontier fortress

Hyksos fortress

Founded 331

Greek trading centre c.620

Hyksos capital c.1730-1570

Merenptah defeats invaders c.1221

Israelite tribes led back to Promised land by Moses (13th century)

Mediterranean Sea

4th millennium settlement

Solar cult-centre

Alexandria

Buto

Avaris

Tjel

Sais

Tanis (Zoan)

Piari
Naucratis

Pernefer

Bubastis
(Bast)

LOWER
EGYPT

Merimdeh-ben-
Salama

Rosetta Br.

Tell-el-Yahudiyeh

Early capital of united Egypt

Giza

Heliopolis

Single state c.3400

MEMPHIS
Sakkara

S I N A I

L.Mareotis

Fayum

Serabet-el-Khadem

□ *Copper Mines*
□ *Turquoise Mines*

Pyramids, 26th century

Libyan

Eastern

EGYPT

Alphabet c.1500

MIDDLE

Desert

Desert

Tell-el-Amarna

Nile

Capital of Akhnaten, c.1370-1352

Ptolemais

Founded by Ptolemy I (d.282)

THEBES

Deir-el-Bahri

Karnak

Capital, early 2nd millennium

UPPER   EGYPT

Ist Cataract

Absorbed lower Egypt c.3200

Horse, c.1900

Abu Simbel

Buhen

2nd Cataract

Nile

The Old Kingdom (c 2700-2180) was the time of the Great Pyramid of Cheops (c 2575). Middle Kingdom: c 2180. Then, after the Hyksos (Asian) interlude, the New Kingdom began in c 1570. Thothmes III reigned in the 15th and Rameses II in the 13th century.

0   100

Miles

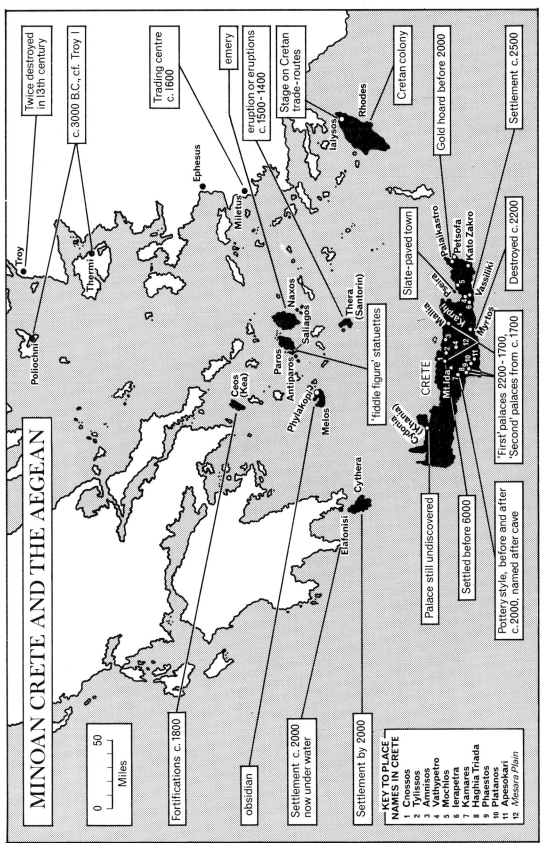

MINOAN CRETE AND THE AEGEAN

Miles
0   50

Twice destroyed in 13th century

c. 3000 B.C., cf. Troy I

Trading centre c. 1600

emery

eruption or eruptions c. 1500–1400

Stage on Cretan trade-routes

Cretan colony

Gold hoard before 2000

Settlement c. 2500

Destroyed c. 2200

Troy

Poliochni

Thermi

Ephesus

Miletus

Rhodes

Ialysos

Naxos

Paros

Antiparos

Saliagos

Ceos (Kea)

Phylakopi

Melos

Thera (Santorin)

Cythera

Elafonisi

'fiddle figure' statuettes

Slate-paved town

Palaikastro

Petsofa

Kato Zakro

Tsera

Vassiliki

Myrtos

Mallia

Karphi

CRETE

Mt. Ida

Cidonia (Khania)

'First' palaces 2200–1700, 'Second' palaces from c. 1700

Palace still undiscovered

Settled before 6000

Pottery style, before and after c. 2000, named after cave

Settlement c. 2000 now under water

obsidian

Fortifications c. 1800

Settlement by 2000

KEY TO PLACE
NAMES IN CRETE
1 Cnossos
2 Tylissos
3 Amnisos
4 Vathypetro
5 Mochlos
6 Ierapetra
7 Kamares
8 Haghia Triada
9 Phaestos
10 Platanos
11 Apesokari
12 *Mesara Plain*

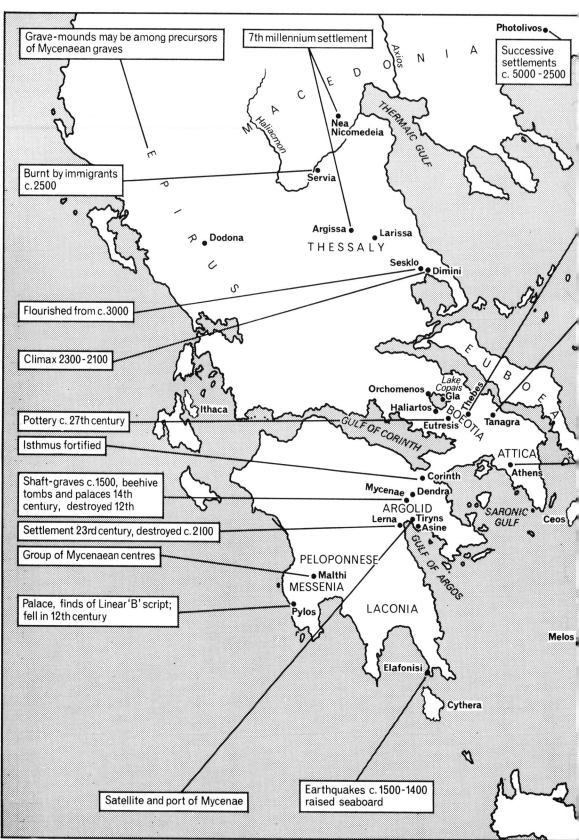

Grave-mounds may be among precursors of Mycenaean graves

7th millennium settlement

Photolivos•

Successive settlements c. 5000 - 2500

Axios

M A C E D O N I A

THERMAIC GULF

Haliacmon

E P I R U S

Nea Nicomedeia•

Burnt by immigrants c. 2500

Servia•

Dodona•

Argissa• Larissa•

THESSALY

Sesklo• •Dimini

Flourished from c. 3000

Climax 2300-2100

E U B O E A

Lake Copais
Orchomenos• •Gla Thebes
Haliartos• BOEOTIA •Tanagra
Eutresis•

Ithaca

Pottery c. 27th century

GULF OF CORINTH

Isthmus fortified

ATTICA

Athens•

•Corinth

Shaft-graves c.1500, beehive tombs and palaces 14th century, destroyed 12th

Mycenae• •Dendra
ARGOLID
Lerna• •Tiryns
•Asine

SARONIC GULF

Ceos

Settlement 23rd century, destroyed c. 2100

Group of Mycenaean centres

PELOPONNESE

MESSENIA

•Malthi

GULF OF ARGOS

Palace, finds of Linear 'B' script; fell in 12th century

Pylos•

LACONIA

Melos•

Elafonisi•

Cythera•

Satellite and port of Mycenae

Earthquakes c. 1500-1400 raised seaboard

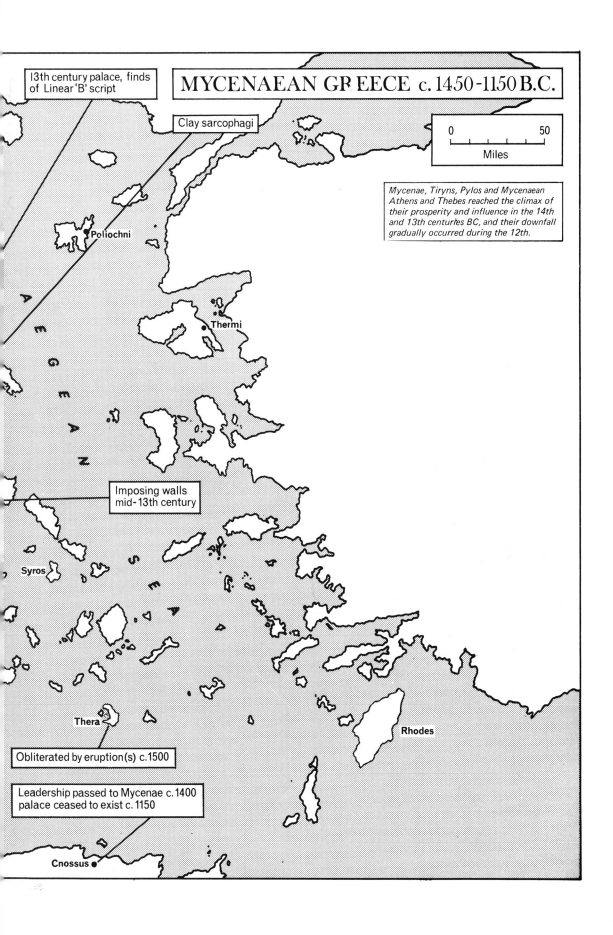

MYCENAEAN GREECE c. 1450-1150 B.C.

13th century palace, finds
of Linear 'B' script

Clay sarcophagi

0   50

Miles

*Mycenae, Tiryns, Pylos and Mycenaean
Athens and Thebes reached the climax of
their prosperity and influence in the 14th
and 13th centuries BC, and their downfall
gradually occurred during the 12th.*

A E G E A N

Poliochni

Thermi

Imposing walls
mid-13th century

S E A

Syros

Thera

Rhodes

Obliterated by eruption(s) c.1500

Leadership passed to Mycenae c.1400
palace ceased to exist c. 1150

Cnossus

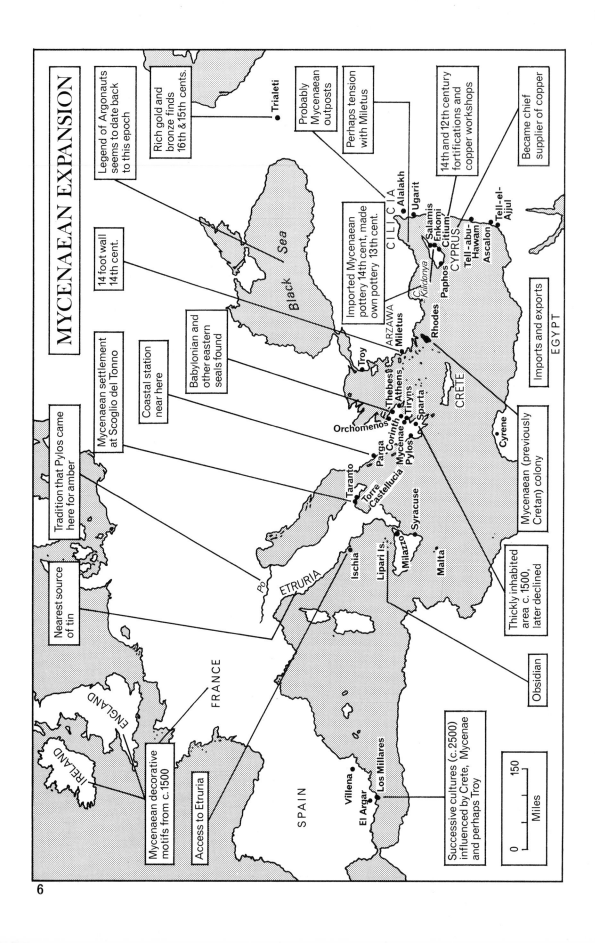

MYCENAEAN EXPANSION

Legend of Argonauts seems to date back to this epoch

Rich gold and bronze finds 16th & 15th cents.

Probably Mycenaean outposts

Perhaps tension with Miletus

14th and 12th century fortifications and copper workshops

Became chief supplier of copper

14 foot wall 14th cent.

Imported Mycenaean pottery 14th cent. made own pottery 13th cent.

Babylonian and other eastern seals found

Mycenaean settlement at Scoglio del Tonno

Coastal station near here

Tradition that Pylos came here for amber

Nearest source of tin

Mycenaean decorative motifs from c.1500

Access to Etruria

Mycenaean (previously Cretan) colony

Thickly inhabited area c. 1500, later declined

Obsidian

Successive cultures (c. 2500) influenced by Crete, Mycenae and perhaps Troy

Trialeti

Black Sea

CILICIA

Ugarit
Alalakh

Salamis
Enkomi
Citium?
Paphos
CYPRUS
Tell-abu-
Hawam
Ascalon
Tell-el-
Ajjul

ARZAWA
Kildonya
Miletus
Rhodes

Troy

Thebes
Athens
Corinth
Tiryns
Mycenae
Sparta
Pylos
Orchomenos

CRETE

Cyrene

Parga

Taranto
Torre
Castellucia
Syracuse
Milazzo
Malta
Lipari Is.
Ischia

_Po_
ETRURIA
FRANCE
ENGLAND
IRELAND

SPAIN
Villena
El Argar
Los Millares

EGYPT

Imports and exports

0   150
Miles

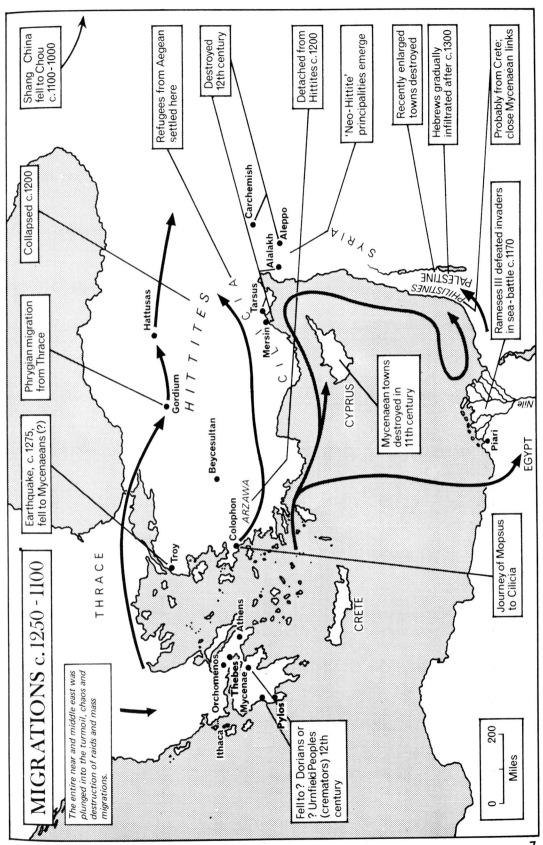

MIGRATIONS c. 1250 - 1100

The entire near and middle east was plunged into the turmoil, chaos and destruction of raids and mass migrations.

Shang China fell to Chou c. 1100 - 1000

Refugees from Aegean settled here

Destroyed 12th century

Detached from Hittites c. 1200

'Neo-Hittite' principalities emerge

Recently enlarged towns destroyed

Hebrews gradually infiltrated after c. 1300

Probably from Crete; close Mycenaean links

Rameses III defeated invaders in sea-battle c. 1170

Collapsed c. 1200

Phrygian migration from Thrace

Earthquake, c. 1275, fell to Mycenaeans (?)

Mycenaean towns destroyed in 11th century

Journey of Mopsus to Cilicia

Fell to ? Dorians or ? Urnfield Peoples (cremators) 12th century

THRACE

Troy

HITTITES

Hattusas

Gordium

Beycesultan

Colophon

ARZAWA

Carchemish

Aleppo

Alalakh

Tarsus

Mersin

C I L I C I A

S Y R I A

PALESTINE

PHILISTINES

CYPRUS

Nile

Piari

EGYPT

CRETE

Ithaca

Orchomenos

Athens

Thebes

Mycenae

Pylos

0   200

Miles

7

PHOENICIAN TRADE & COLONISATION

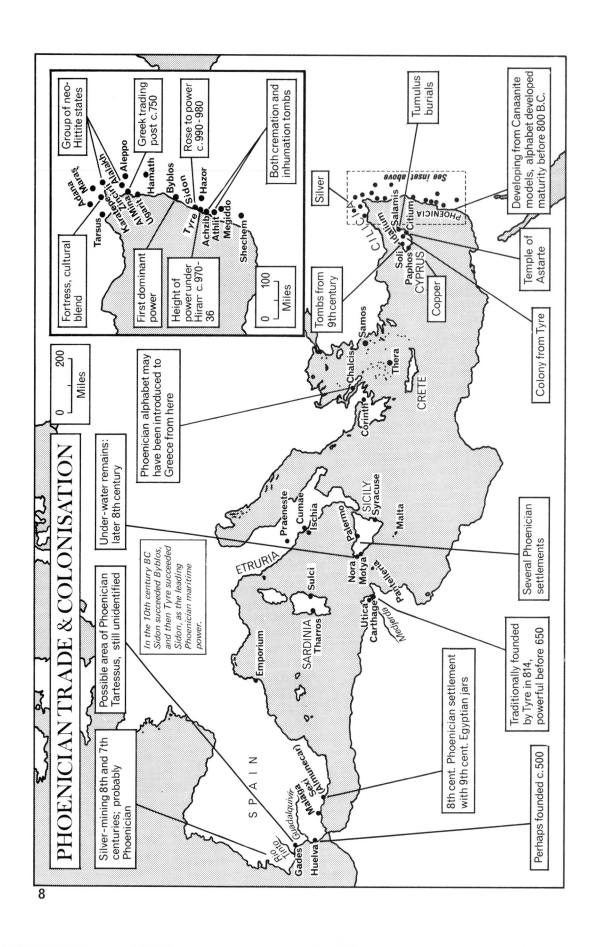

Silver-mining 8th and 7th centuries; probably Phoenician

Possible area of Phoenician Tartessus, still unidentified

Under-water remains: later 8th century

In the 10th century BC Sidon succeeded Byblos, and then Tyre succeeded Sidon, as the leading Phoenician maritime power.

Phoenician alphabet may have been introduced to Greece from here

Several Phoenician settlements

8th cent. Phoenician settlement with 9th cent. Egyptian jars

Traditionally founded by Tyre in 814, powerful before 650

Perhaps founded c.500

0   200
Miles

Inset map

Group of neo-Hittite states

Greek trading post c.750

Rose to power c.990 – 980

Both cremation and inhumation tombs

Fortress, cultural blend

First dominant power

Height of power under Hiram c.970 – 36

Tombs from 9th century

Silver

Tumulus burials

Developing from Canaanite models, alphabet developed maturity before 800 B.C.

Temple of Astarte

Colony from Tyre

Copper

0   100
Miles

Inset place names

Adana, Maraş, Tarsus, Karatepe, Alalakh, Al Mina, Ugarit, Aleppo, Hamath, Byblos, Sidon, Tyre, Hazor, Achzib, Athlit, Megiddo, Shechem

Main map place names

PHOENICIA, CILICIA, Soli, Salamis, Paphos, CYPRUS, Citium, Chalcis, Samos, Corinth, Thera, CRETE, Cumae, Praeneste, Ischia, Palermo, SICILY, Syracuse, Malta, ETRURIA, Sulci, Nora, Motya, Pantelleria, Emporium, SARDINIA, Tharros, Utica, Carthage, Medjerda, S P A I N, Guadalquivir, Málaga, Sexi (Almuñecar), Rio Tinto, Gades, Huelva

8

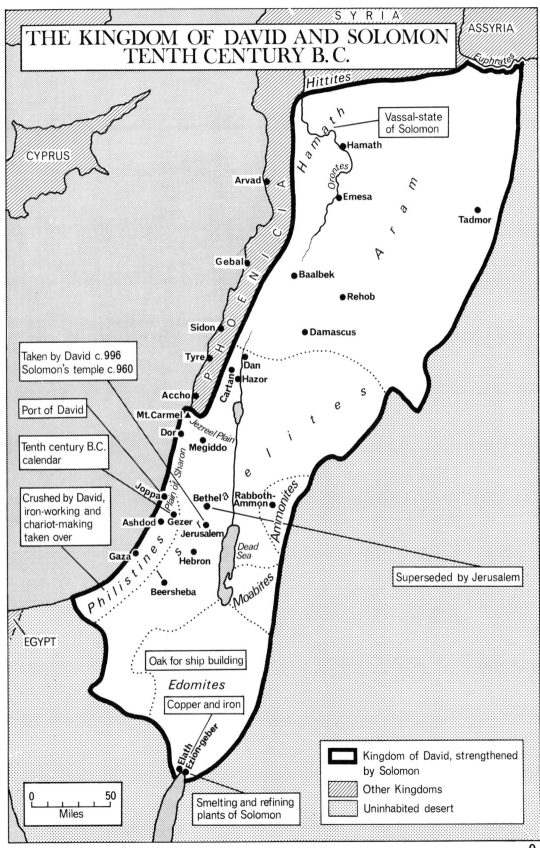

THE KINGDOM OF DAVID AND SOLOMON TENTH CENTURY B.C.

SYRIA

ASSYRIA

Euphrates

CYPRUS

Hittites

H a m a t h

Vassal-state of Solomon

Hamath

Orontes

Arvad

Emesa

A r a m

Tadmor

Gebal

Baalbek

Rehob

Sidon

Damascus

Taken by David c.996
Solomon's temple c.960

Tyre

Dan

Cartan

Hazor

Accho

Mt. Carmel

Port of David

Dor

Jezreel Plain

Megiddo

I s r a e l i t e s

Tenth century B.C.
calendar

Plain of Sharon

Joppa

Bethel

Rabboth-Ammon

Ammonites

Crushed by David,
iron-working and
chariot-making
taken over

Ashdod

Gezer

Jerusalem

Superseded by Jerusalem

Gaza

Hebron

Dead
Sea

P h i l i s t i n e s

Moabites

Beersheba

EGYPT

Oak for ship building

Edomites

Copper and iron

Elath
Ezion-geber

| | 0 | | 50 | |
| Miles |

Smelting and refining
plants of Solomon

Kingdom of David, strengthened
by Solomon

Other Kingdoms

Uninhabited desert

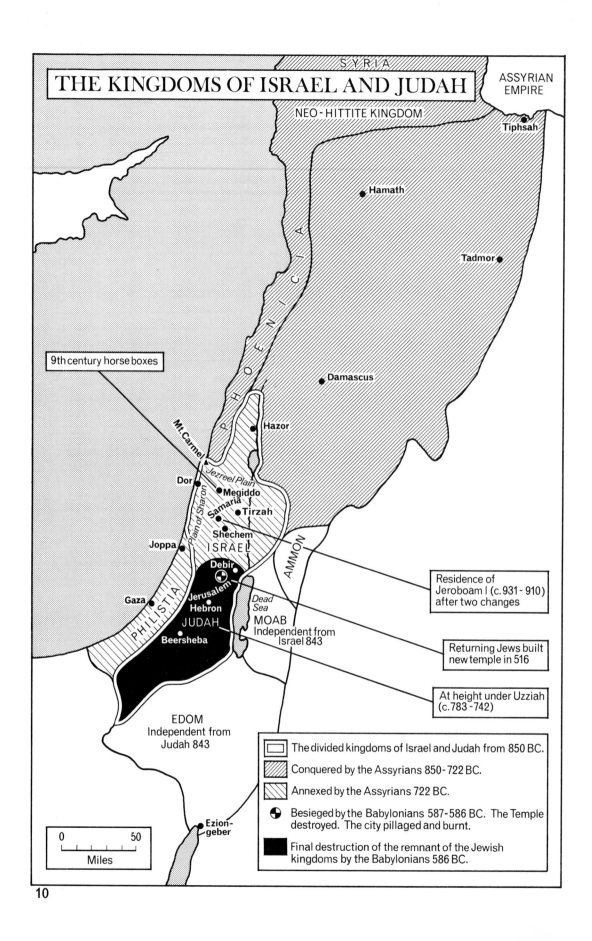

THE KINGDOMS OF ISRAEL AND JUDAH

SYRIA

ASSYRIAN EMPIRE

NEO - HITTITE KINGDOM

Tiphsah

Hamath

Tadmor

PHOENICIA

9th century horse boxes

Damascus

Mt. Carmel

Hazor

Jezreel Plain

Dor

Megiddo

Plain of Sharon

Samaria

Tirzah

Shechem

Joppa

ISRAEL

AMMON

Debir

Jerusalem

Hebron

Dead Sea

Gaza

PHILISTIA

JUDAH

MOAB
Independent from Israel 843

Beersheba

Residence of Jeroboam I (c. 931 - 910) after two changes

Returning Jews built new temple in 516

At height under Uzziah (c. 783 - 742)

EDOM
Independent from Judah 843

Eziongeber

0   50

Miles

The divided kingdoms of Israel and Judah from 850 BC.

Conquered by the Assyrians 850 - 722 BC.

Annexed by the Assyrians 722 BC.

Besieged by the Babylonians 587 - 586 BC. The Temple destroyed. The city pillaged and burnt.

Final destruction of the remnant of the Jewish kingdoms by the Babylonians 586 BC.

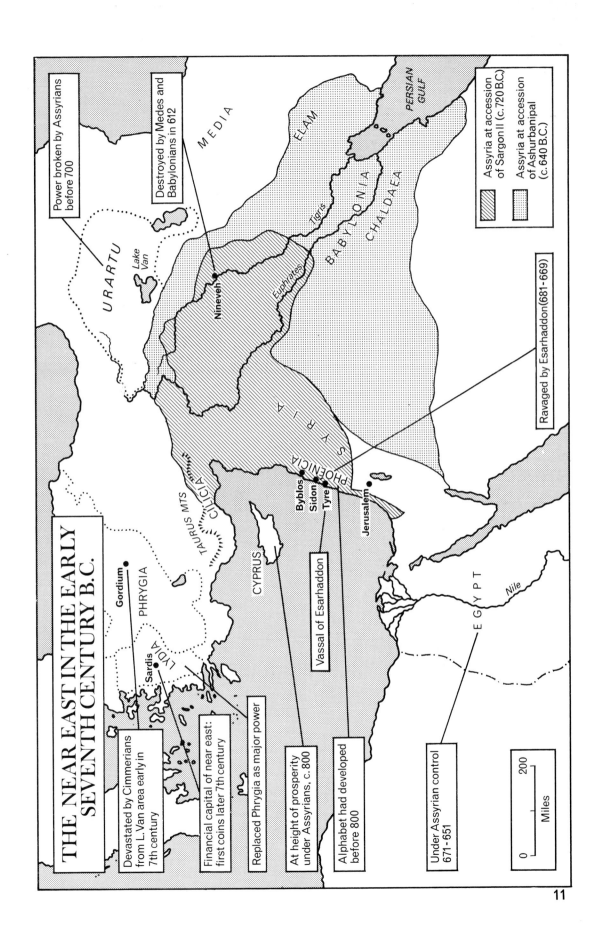

THE NEAR EAST IN THE EARLY
SEVENTH CENTURY B.C.

Power broken by Assyrians before 700

Destroyed by Medes and Babylonians in 612

Assyria at accession of Sargon II (c. 720 B.C.)

Assyria at accession of Ashurbanipal (c. 640 B.C.)

Ravaged by Esarhaddon (681-669)

MEDIA

ELAM

PERSIAN GULF

URARTU

Lake Van

BABYLONIA

CHALDAEA

Tigris

Nineveh

Euphrates

A S S Y R I A

TAURUS MTS

CILICIA

PHOENICIA

S Y R I A

Byblos

Sidon

Tyre

Jerusalem

CYPRUS

LYDIA

Sardis

Gordium

PHRYGIA

E G Y P T

Nile

Devastated by Cimmerians from L. Van area early in 7th century

Financial capital of near east: first coins later 7th century

Replaced Phrygia as major power

At height of prosperity under Assyrians, c. 800

Alphabet had developed before 800

Vassal of Esarhaddon

Under Assyrian control 671-651

0   200

Miles

11

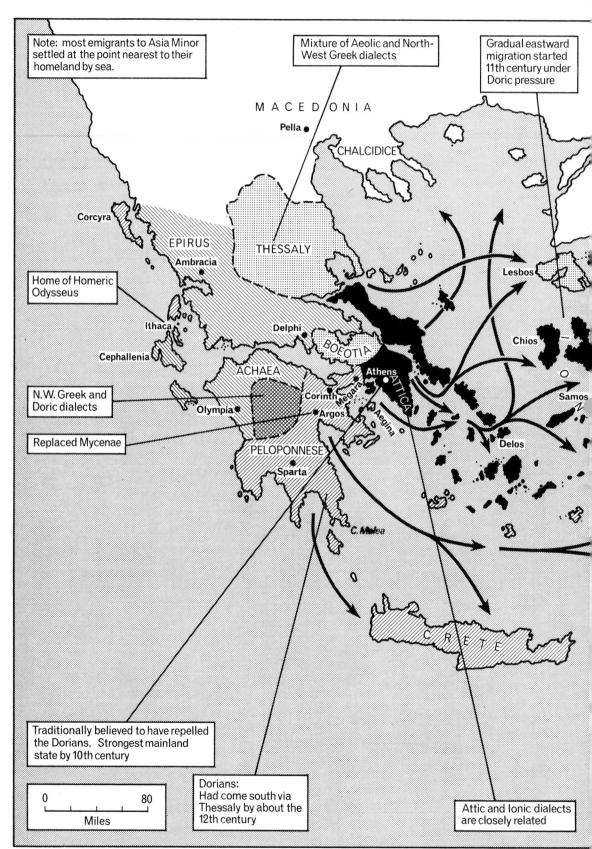

Note: most emigrants to Asia Minor settled at the point nearest to their homeland by sea.

Mixture of Aeolic and North-West Greek dialects

Gradual eastward migration started 11th century under Doric pressure

M A C E D O N I A

Pella •

CHALCIDICE

Corcyra

EPIRUS

Ambracia

THESSALY

Lesbos

Home of Homeric Odysseus

Ithaca

Delphi

BOEOTIA

Chios

Cephallenia

ACHAEA

Athens

ATTICA

Samos

N.W. Greek and Doric dialects

Corinth

Megara

Olympia •

Argos

Aegina

Replaced Mycenae

Delos

PELOPONNESE

Sparta

C. Malea

Traditionally believed to have repelled the Dorians. Strongest mainland state by 10th century

C R E T E

0   80

Miles

Dorians:
Had come south via Thessaly by about the 12th century

Attic and Ionic dialects are closely related

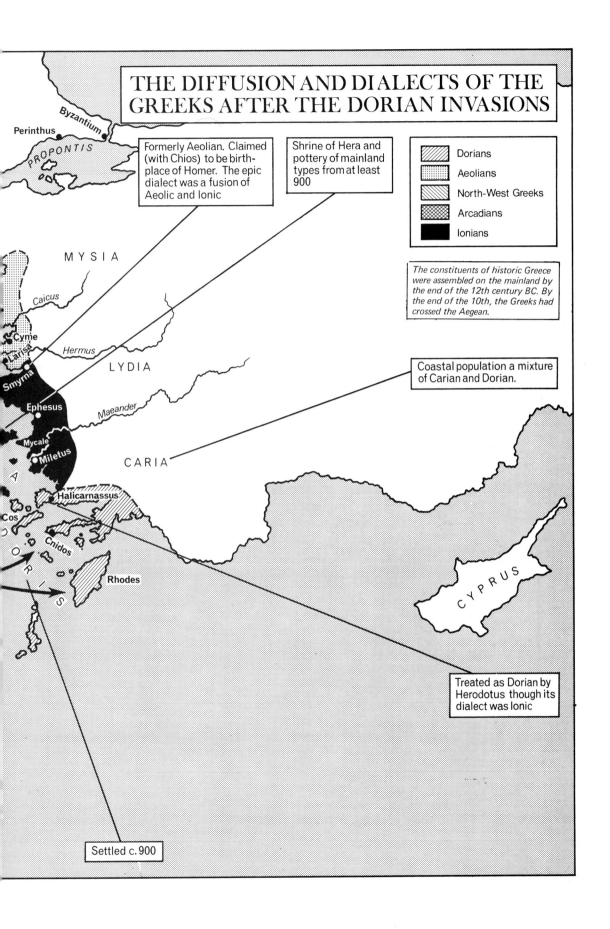

THE DIFFUSION AND DIALECTS OF THE GREEKS AFTER THE DORIAN INVASIONS

Formerly Aeolian. Claimed (with Chios) to be birth-place of Homer. The epic dialect was a fusion of Aeolic and Ionic

Shrine of Hera and pottery of mainland types from at least 900

Dorians
Aeolians
North-West Greeks
Arcadians
Ionians

The constituents of historic Greece were assembled on the mainland by the end of the 12th century BC. By the end of the 10th, the Greeks had crossed the Aegean.

Coastal population a mixture of Carian and Dorian.

Treated as Dorian by Herodotus though its dialect was Ionic

Settled c. 900

Perinthus

Byzantium

PROPONTIS

MYSIA

Caicus

Cyme

Larisa

Hermus

LYDIA

Smyrna

Ephesus

Maeander

Mycale

Miletus

CARIA

Halicarnassus

Cos

Cnidos

DORIS

Rhodes

CYPRUS

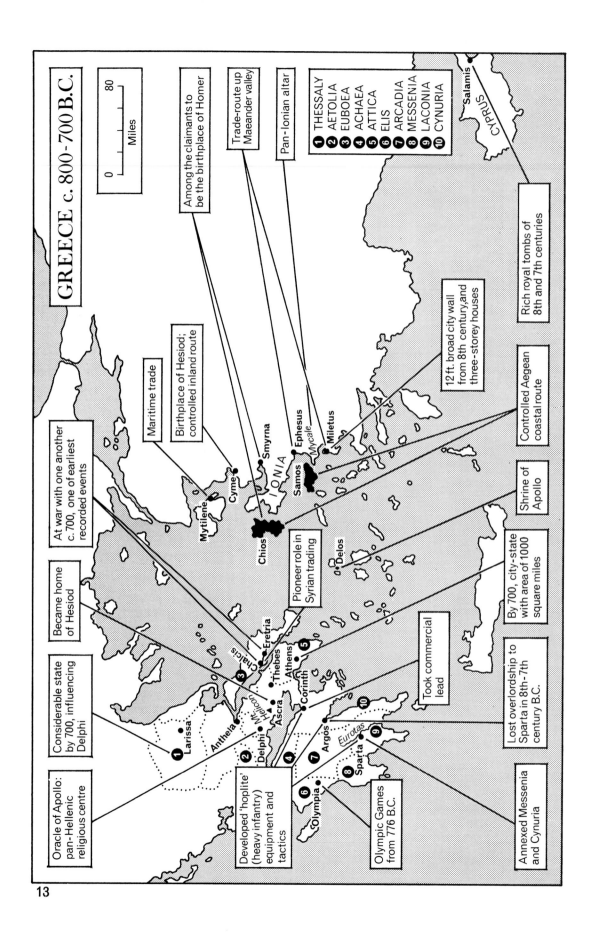

GREECE c. 800 - 700 B.C.

0 [scale] 80
Miles

❶	THESSALY
❷	AETOLIA
❸	EUBOEA
❹	ACHAEA
❺	ATTICA
❻	ELIS
❼	ARCADIA
❽	MESSENIA
❾	LACONIA
❿	CYNURIA

Among the claimants to be the birthplace of Homer

Trade-route up Maeander valley

Pan-Ionian altar

Maritime trade

Birthplace of Hesiod; controlled inland route

At war with one another c. 700, one of earliest recorded events

Became home of Hesiod

Considerable state by 700, influencing Delphi

Oracle of Apollo: pan-Hellenic religious centre

Developed 'hoplite' (heavy infantry) equipment and tactics

Olympic Games from 776 B.C.

Annexed Messenia and Cynuria

Lost overlordship to Sparta in 8th - 7th century B.C.

By 700, city-state with area of 1000 square miles

Took commercial lead

Shrine of Apollo

Controlled Aegean coastal route

12 ft. broad city wall from 8th century, and three-storey houses

Rich royal tombs of 8th and 7th centuries

Pioneer role in Syrian trading

CYPRUS

Salamis

Smyrna
Ephesus
Miletus
Mycale
Samos
I O N I A
Cyme
Mytilene
Chios
Delos

Eretria
Chalcis
Thebes
Athens ❺
Corinth
Larissa ❶
Anthela
Delphi ❷ Ascra
Helicon
Mt.
Olympia ❻
Argos ❼
Eurotas
Sparta ❽
❾
❿
❹
❸

13

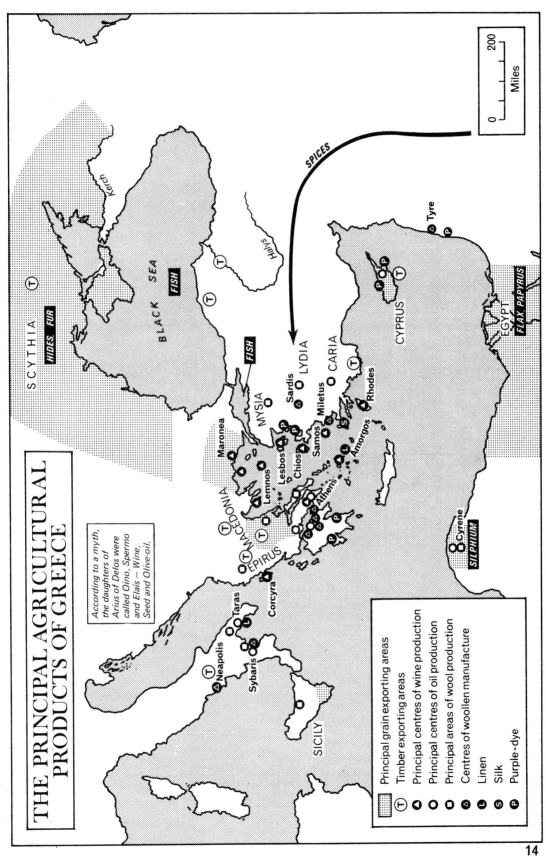

THE PRINCIPAL AGRICULTURAL PRODUCTS OF GREECE

According to a myth, the daughters of Arius of Delos were called Oino, Spermo and Elais – Wine, Seed and Olive-oil.

S C Y T H I A

HIDES **FUR**

Kerch

B L A C K   S E A

FISH

Halys

FISH

SPICES

Tyre

CYPRUS

FLAX PAPYRUS

EGYPT

MYSIA

Sardis

LYDIA

Maronea

Miletus

CARIA

Rhodes

Lesbos

Chios

Samos

Amorgos

Lemnos

MACEDONIA

Athens

EPIRUS

Cyrene

SILPHIUM

Corcyra

Taras

Neapolis

Sybaris

SICILY

0   200
Miles

⬚ (shaded)	Principal grain exporting areas
Ⓣ	Timber exporting areas
◀	Principal centres of wine production
◯	Principal centres of oil production
▢	Principal areas of wool production
◬	Centres of woollen manufacture
Ⓛ	Linen
Ⓢ	Silk
Ⓟ	Purple-dye

14

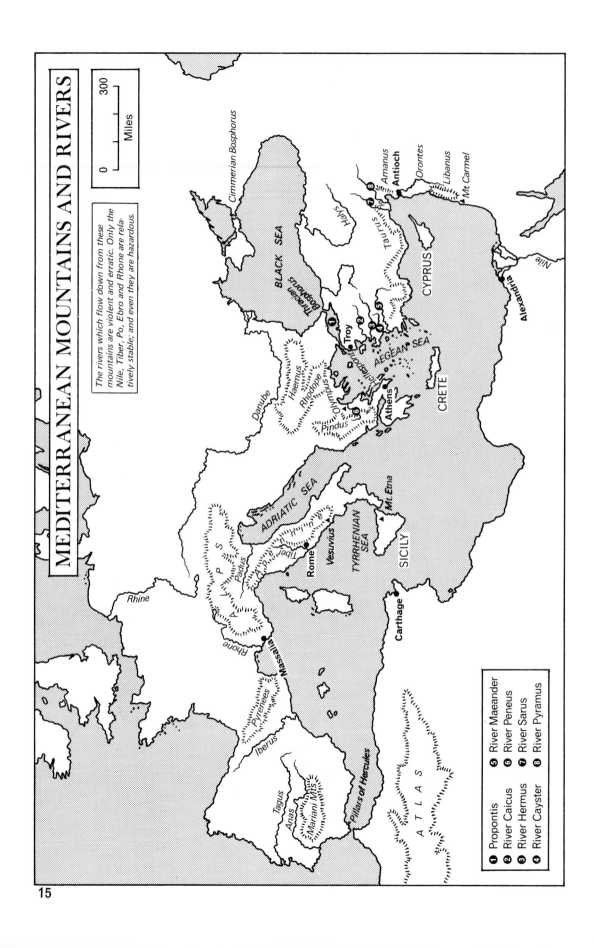

MEDITERRANEAN MOUNTAINS AND RIVERS

The rivers which flow down from these mountains are violent and erratic. Only the Nile, Tiber, Po, Ebro and Rhone are relatively stable; and even they are hazardous.

0   300
Miles

1 Propontis   **5** River Maeander
2 River Caicus   **6** River Peneus
3 River Hermus   **7** River Sarus
4 River Cayster   **8** River Pyramus

Cimmerian Bosphorus

Amanus
Antioch
Orontes
Libanus
Mt Carmel

Taurus

CYPRUS

BLACK SEA

Thracian Bosphorus

Halys

Nile

Alexandria

Troy

Hellespont

AEGEAN SEA

Danube

Haemus

Rhodope

Olympus

Pindus

Athens

CRETE

ADRIATIC SEA

A L P S

Padus

Tiber

Apennines

Rome

Vesuvius

M. Etna

TYRRHENIAN SEA

SICILY

Rhine

Rhone

Massalia

Pyrenees

Iberus

Carthage

Tagus

Anas

Mariani Mts

Pillars of Hercules

A T L A S

RAINFALL IN THE MEDITERRANEAN AREA

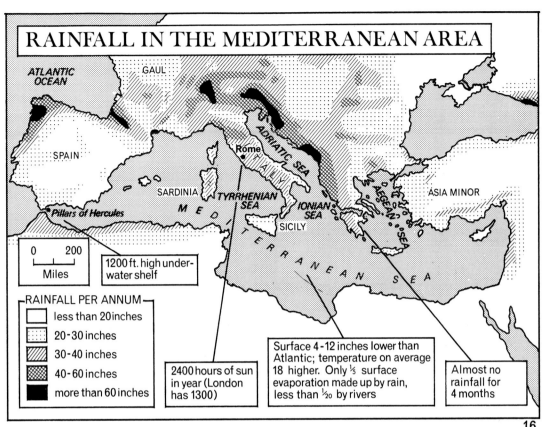

ATLANTIC OCEAN

GAUL

SPAIN

SARDINIA

TYRRHENIAN SEA

Rome

ADRIATIC SEA

IONIAN SEA

SICILY

AEGEAN SEA

ASIA MINOR

Pillars of Hercules

MEDITERRANEAN SEA

0   200
Miles

1200 ft. high under-water shelf

RAINFALL PER ANNUM
- less than 20 inches
- 20-30 inches
- 30-40 inches
- 40-60 inches
- more than 60 inches

2400 hours of sun in year (London has 1300)

Surface 4-12 inches lower than Atlantic; temperature on average 18 higher. Only ⅓ surface evaporation made up by rain, less than ¹⁄₂₀ by rivers

Almost no rainfall for 4 months

MINERALS IN THE EASTERN MEDITERRANEAN AREA

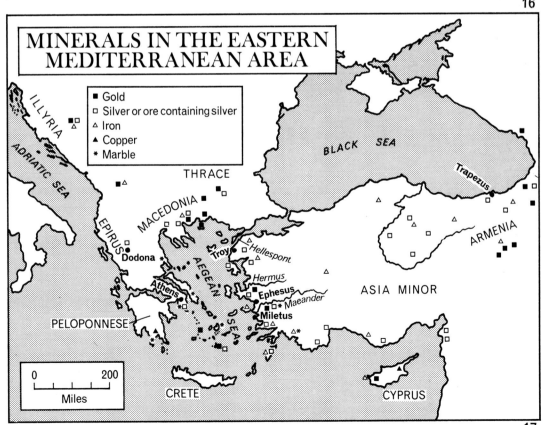

- ■ Gold
- □ Silver or ore containing silver
- △ Iron
- ▲ Copper
- * Marble

ILLYRIA

ADRIATIC SEA

EPIRUS

THRACE

MACEDONIA

BLACK SEA

Trapezus

ARMENIA

Dodona

Troy

Hellespont

Hermus

Athens

AEGEAN SEA

Ephesus

Maeander

Miletus

ASIA MINOR

PELOPONNESE

CRETE

CYPRUS

0   200
Miles

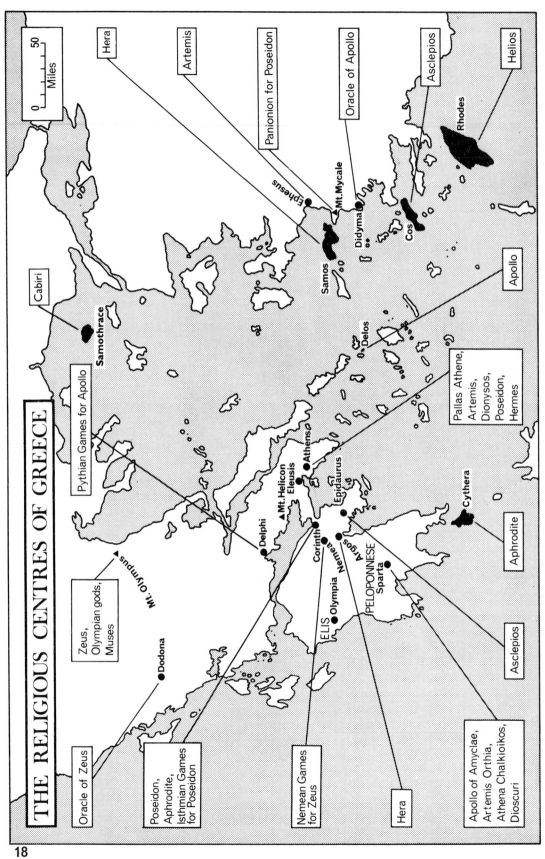

THE RELIGIOUS CENTRES OF GREECE

Oracle of Zeus

Hera

Artemis

Panionion for Poseidon

Oracle of Apollo

Asclepios

Helios

Cabiri

Pythian Games for Apollo

Apollo

Pallas Athene, Artemis, Dionysos, Poseidon, Hermes

Zeus, Olympian gods, Muses

Poseidon, Aphrodite, Isthmian Games for Poseidon

Aphrodite

Asclepios

Nemean Games for Zeus

Hera

Apollo of Amyclae, Artemis Orthia, Athena Chalkioikos, Dioscuri

50
Miles
0

Rhodes

Ephesus

Mt. Mycale

Didyma

Cos

Samos

Samothrace

Delos

Mt. Olympus

Dodona

Delphi

▲Mt. Helicon
Eleusis

Athens

Epidaurus

Cythera

Corinth

Nemea

Argos

ELIS

Olympia

PELOPONNESE

Sparta

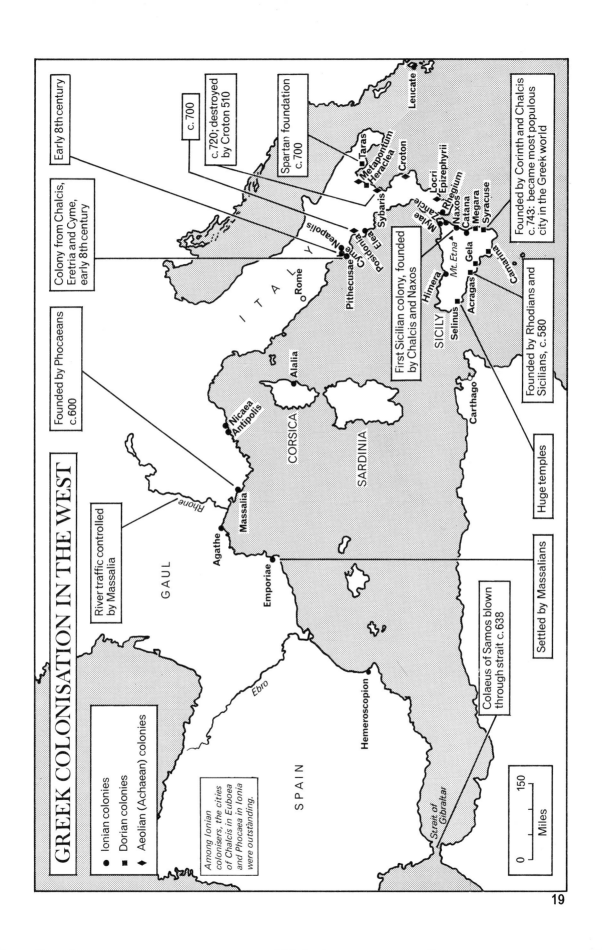

GREEK COLONISATION IN THE WEST

Ionian colonies ●
Dorian colonies ■
Aeolian (Achaean) colonies ◆

Among Ionian colonisers, the cities of Chalcis in Euboea and Phocaea in Ionia were outstanding.

Early 8th century

c. 700

c. 720; destroyed by Croton 510

Spartan foundation c. 700

Colony from Chalcis, Eretria and Cyme, early 8th century

Founded by Corinth and Chalcis c. 743: became most populous city in the Greek world

Founded by Phocaeans c. 600

First Sicilian colony, founded by Chalcis and Naxos

Founded by Rhodians and Sicilians, c. 580

River traffic controlled by Massalia

Huge temples

Settled by Massalians

Colaeus of Samos blown through strait c. 638

Leucate

Taras
Metapontum
Heraclea
Croton
Sybaris
Locri Epizephyrii
Rhegium
Myiae
Mylae
Naxos
Catana
Megara
Syracuse
Posidonia
Elea
Cyme
Neapolis
Pithecusae
Rome
ITALY
Himera
Mt. Etna
Gela
Acragas
Selinus
SICILY
Camarina

Alalia
CORSICA
SARDINIA
Carthago
Carthago

Nicaea
Antipolis
Massalia
Agathe
Emporiae
Rhone
GAUL

Ebro
Hemeroscopion
SPAIN
Strait of Gibraltar

0   150
Miles

19

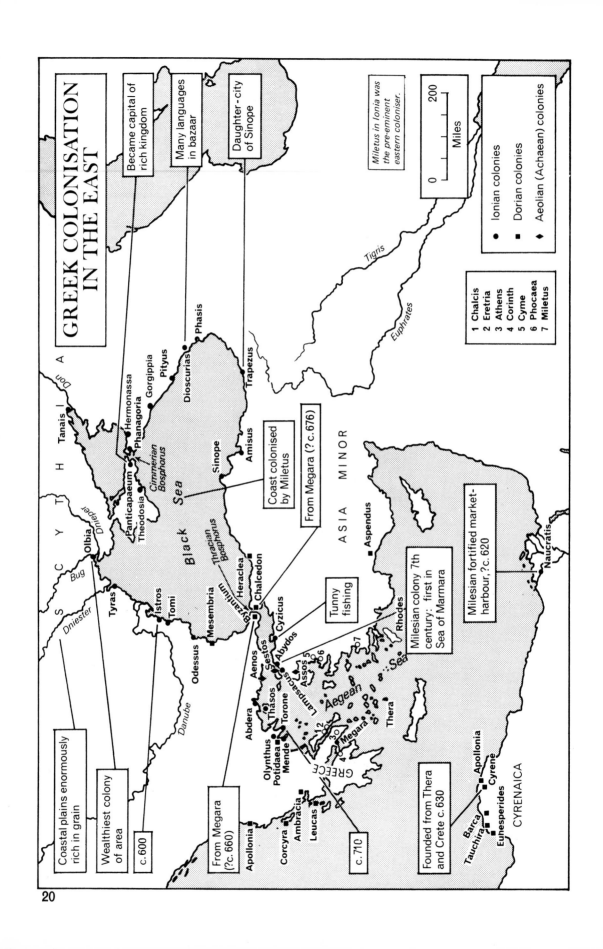

GREEK COLONISATION IN THE EAST

Miletus in Ionia was the pre-eminent eastern coloniser.

- ● Ionian colonies
- ■ Dorian colonies
- ◆ Aeolian (Achaean) colonies

1 Chalcis
2 Eretria
3 Athens
4 Corinth
5 Cyme
6 Phocaea
7 Miletus

0   200
Miles

Became capital of rich kingdom

Many languages in bazaar

Daughter-city of Sinope

Coast colonised by Miletus

From Megara (?c. 676)

Tunny fishing

Milesian colony 7th century: first in Sea of Marmara

Milesian fortified market-harbour, ?c. 620

Coastal plains enormously rich in grain

Wealthiest colony of area

c. 600

From Megara (?c. 660)

c. 710

Founded from Thera and Crete c. 630

Tigris

Euphrates

S C Y T H I A

Don

Tanais

Hermonassa
Phanagoria
Gorgippia
Pityus
Dioscurias
Phasis

Panticapaeum
Theodosia
Cimmerian Bosphorus

Sinope
Amisus
Trapezus

Black Sea

Dnieper

Olbia
Bug
Dniester

Tyras

Istros
Tomi

Odessus
Mesembria

Thracian Bosphorus
Heraclea
Chalcedon
Byzantium

Cyzicus
Abydos
Sestos
Aenos
Lampsacus
Assos 5
6
7

Abdera
Thasos
Torone
Olynthus
Potidaea
Mende

1 2
3
4

Megara

Thera

A S I A   M I N O R

Aspendus

Rhodes

Aegean Sea

G R E E C E

Apollonia
Corcyra
Ambracia
Leucas

Danube

Naucratis

Apollonia
Cyrene
Barca
Tauchira
Euhesperides

CYRENAICA

20

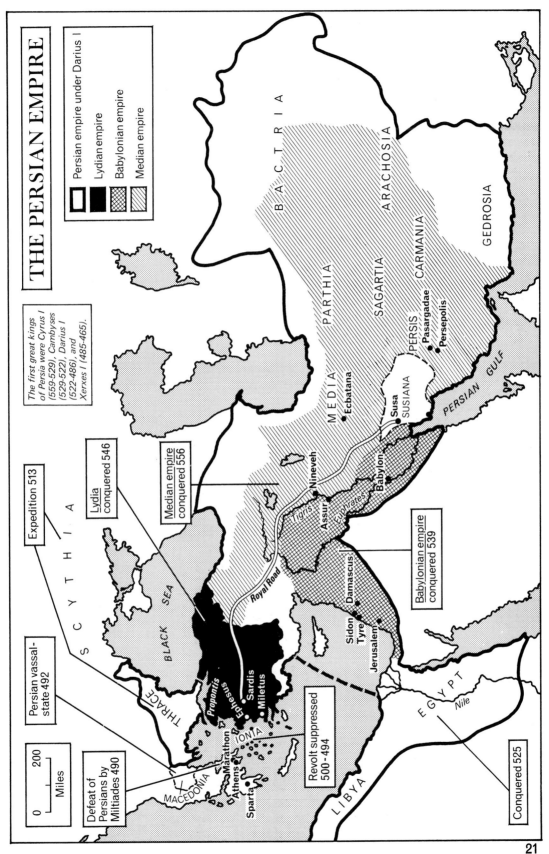

THE PERSIAN EMPIRE

Persian empire under Darius I
Lydian empire
Babylonian empire
Median empire

The first great kings of Persia were Cyrus I (559-529), Cambyses (529-522), Darius I (522-486), and Xerxes I (485-465).

Expedition 513

Lydia conquered 546

Median empire conquered 556

Persian vassal-state 492

Babylonian empire conquered 539

Defeat of Persians by Miltiades 490

Revolt suppressed 500 - 494

Conquered 525

200

Miles

0

SCYTHIA

BLACK SEA

THRACE

MACEDONIA

Athens

Sparta

Marathon

IONIA

Propontis

Ephesus

Sardis

Miletus

Royal Road

Sidon

Tyre

Damascus

Jerusalem

EGYPT

Nile

LIBYA

Nineveh

Assur

Tigris

Euphrates

Babylon

Ecbatana

MEDIA

Susa

SUSIANA

PERSIS

Pasargadae

Persepolis

PERSIAN GULF

PARTHIA

SAGARTIA

ARACHOSIA

CARMANIA

GEDROSIA

BACTRIA

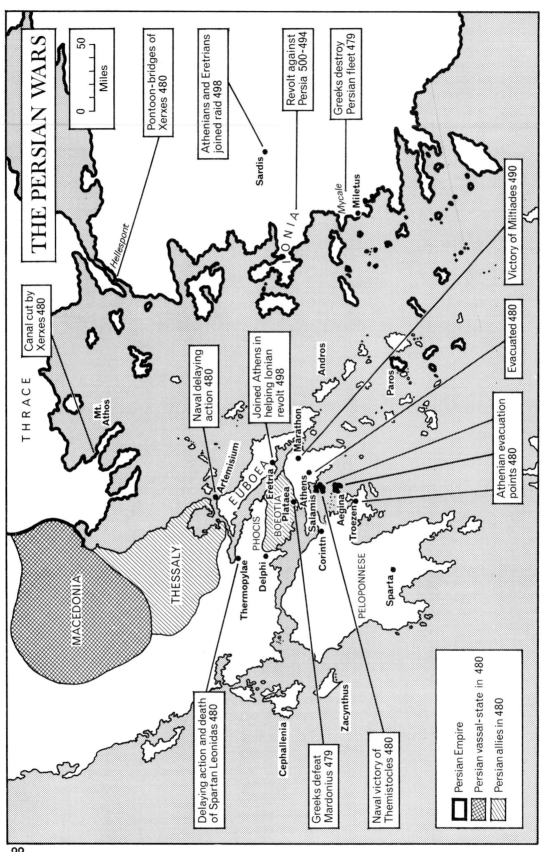

THE PERSIAN WARS

Miles
0   50

Pontoon-bridges of Xerxes 480

Athenians and Eretrians joined raid 498

Revolt against Persia 500-494

Greeks destroy Persian fleet 479

Canal cut by Xerxes 480

THRACE

Mt. Athos

Naval delaying action 480

Joined Athens in helping Ionian revolt 498

Hellespont

Sardis

IONIA

Mycale

Miletus

Victory of Miltiades 490

MACEDONIA

THESSALY

Artemisium

EUBOEA

PHOCIS

BOEOTIA

Plataea

Marathon

Andros

Paros

Evacuated 480

Thermopylae

Delphi

Eretria

Athens

Corinth

Salamis

Aegina

Troezen

PELOPONNESE

Athenian evacuation points 480

Delaying action and death of Spartan Leonidas 480

Cephallenia

Zacynthus

Sparta

Greeks defeat Mardonius 479

Naval victory of Themistocles 480

Persian Empire

Persian vassal-state in 480

Persian allies in 480

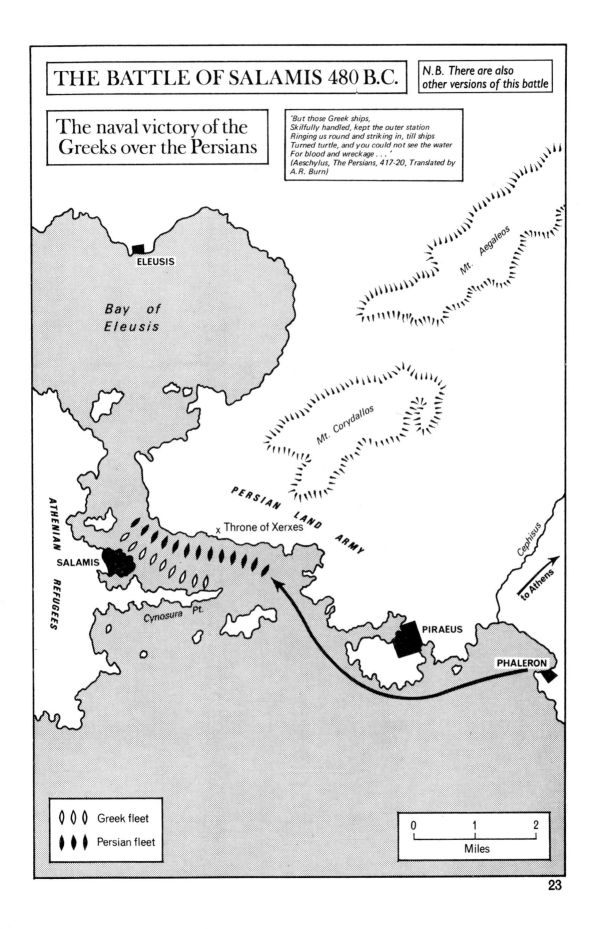

THE BATTLE OF SALAMIS 480 B.C.

N.B. There are also other versions of this battle

The naval victory of the Greeks over the Persians

'But those Greek ships,
Skilfully handled, kept the outer station
Ringing us round and striking in, till ships
Turned turtle, and you could not see the water
For blood and wreckage . . . '
(Aeschylus, The Persians, 417-20, Translated by A.R. Burn)

ELEUSIS

Bay of Eleusis

Mt. Aegaleos

Mt. Corydallos

PERSIAN LAND ARMY

x Throne of Xerxes

Cephisus

to Athens

ATHENIAN REFUGEES

SALAMIS

Cynosura Pt.

PIRAEUS

PHALERON

◊ ◊ ◊   Greek fleet

♦ ♦ ♦   Persian fleet

0   1   2
Miles

23

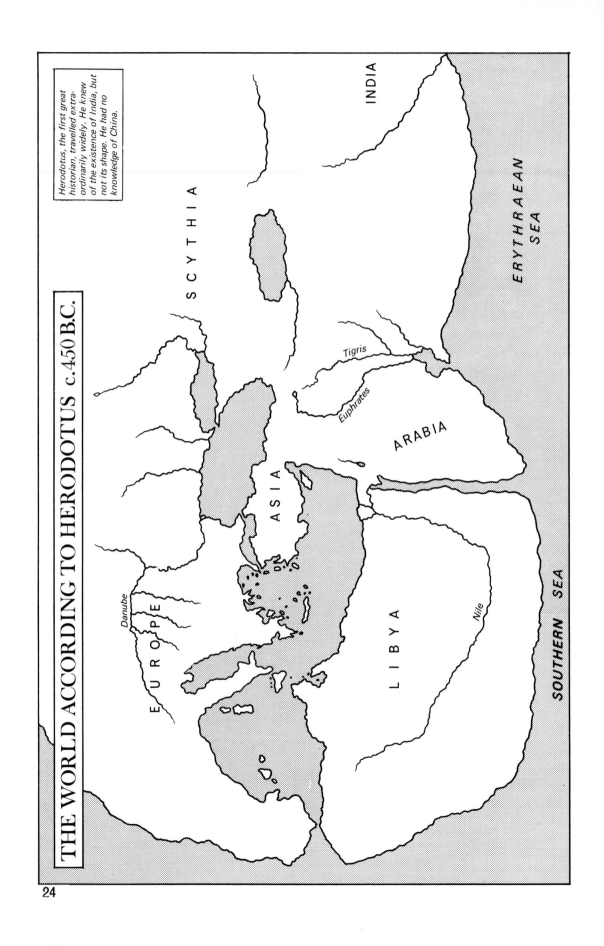

THE WORLD ACCORDING TO HERODOTUS c.450 B.C.

Herodotus, the first great historian, travelled extraordinarily widely. He knew of the existence of India, but not its shape. He had no knowledge of China.

SCYTHIA

INDIA

ERYTHRAEAN SEA

Tigris

Euphrates

ARABIA

ASIA

EUROPE

Danube

LIBYA

Nile

SOUTHERN SEA

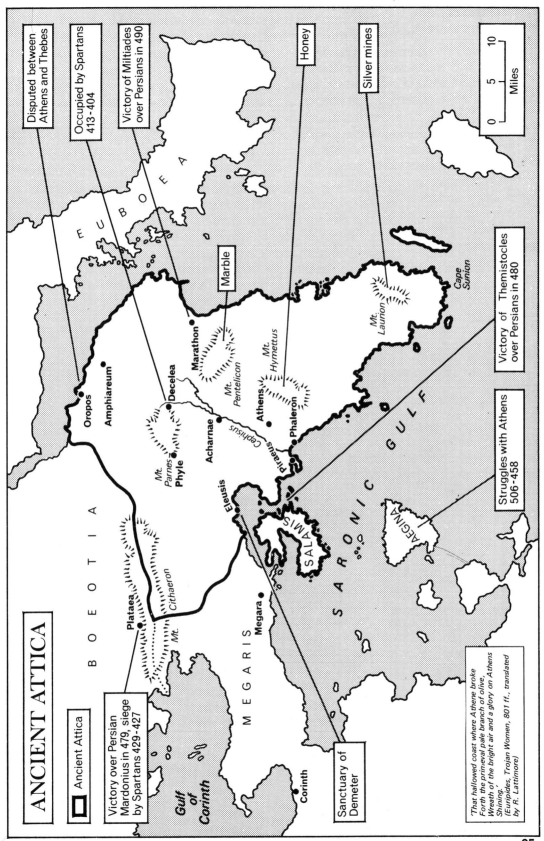

ANCIENT ATTICA

☐ Ancient Attica

Disputed between Athens and Thebes

Occupied by Spartans 413-404

Victory of Miltiades over Persians in 490

Honey

Silver mines

Marble

Victory over Persian Mardonius in 479, siege by Spartans 429-427

Victory of Themistocles over Persians in 480

Struggles with Athens 506-458

Sanctuary of Demeter

'That hallowed coast where Athene broke
Forth the primeval pale branch of olive,
Wreath of the bright air and a glory on Athens
Shining.'
(Euripides, Trojan Women, 801 ff., translated
by R. Lattimore)

EUBOEA

BOEOTIA

MEGARIS

Gulf of Corinth

SARONIC GULF

SALAMIS

AEGINA

Cape Sunion

Oropos

Amphiareum

Decelea

Marathon

Mt. Parnes

Phyle

Acharnae

Mt. Pentelicon

Athens

Mt. Hymettus

Phaleron

Piraeus

Cephisus

Eleusis

Plataea

Mt. Cithaeron

Megara

Corinth

Mt. Laurion

Miles
0   5   10

25

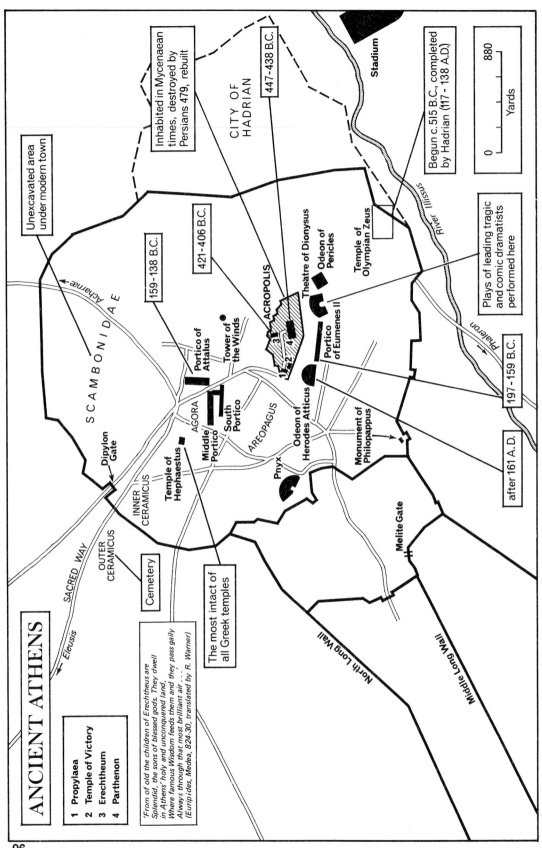

ANCIENT ATHENS

1 Propylaea
2 Temple of Victory
3 Erechtheum
4 Parthenon

"From of old the children of Erechtheus are
Splendid, the sons of blessed gods. They dwell
in Athens' holy and unconquered land,
Where famous Wisdom feeds them and they pass gaily
Always through that most brilliant air . . ."
(Euripides, Medea, 824-30, translated by R. Warner)

Cemetery

The most intact of all Greek temples

Unexcavated area under modern town

Inhabited in Mycenaean times, destroyed by Persians 479, rebuilt

159 - 138 B.C.

421 - 406 B.C.

447-438 B.C.

Begun c. 515 B.C., completed by Hadrian (117 - 138 A.D.)

Plays of leading tragic and comic dramatists performed here

197 - 159 B.C.

after 161 A.D.

SACRED WAY

Eleusis

OUTER CERAMICUS

INNER CERAMICUS

Dipylon Gate

Acharnae

S C A M B O N I D A E

Temple of Hephaestus

AGORA

Middle Portico

South Portico

Portico of Attalus

Tower of the Winds

AREOPAGUS

Pnyx

Odeon of Herodes Atticus

Portico of Eumenes II

ACROPOLIS

Theatre of Dionysus

Odeon of Pericles

Temple of Olympian Zeus

CITY OF HADRIAN

Stadium

River Ilissus

Phaleron

Monument of Philopappus

Melite Gate

North Long Wall

Middle Long Wall

0   880

Yards

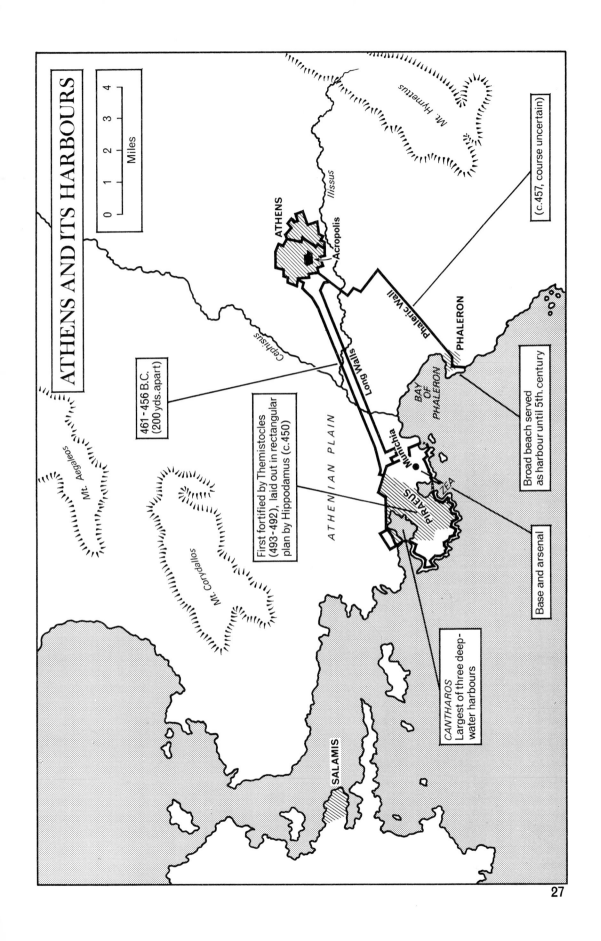

ATHENS AND ITS HARBOURS

Miles
0 1 2 3 4

Mt. Hymettus

Ilissus

ATHENS

Acropolis

(c. 457, course uncertain)

Phaleric Wall

PHALERON

BAY OF PHALERON

Broad beach served as harbour until 5th. century

461 - 456 B.C. (200 yds. apart)

Cephisus

Long Walls

Munichia

ZEA

Base and arsenal

First fortified by Themistocles (493-492), laid out in rectangular plan by Hippodamus (c.450)

Mt. Aegaleos

ATHENIAN PLAIN

PIRAEUS

Mt. Corydallos

CANTHAROS Largest of three deep-water harbours

SALAMIS

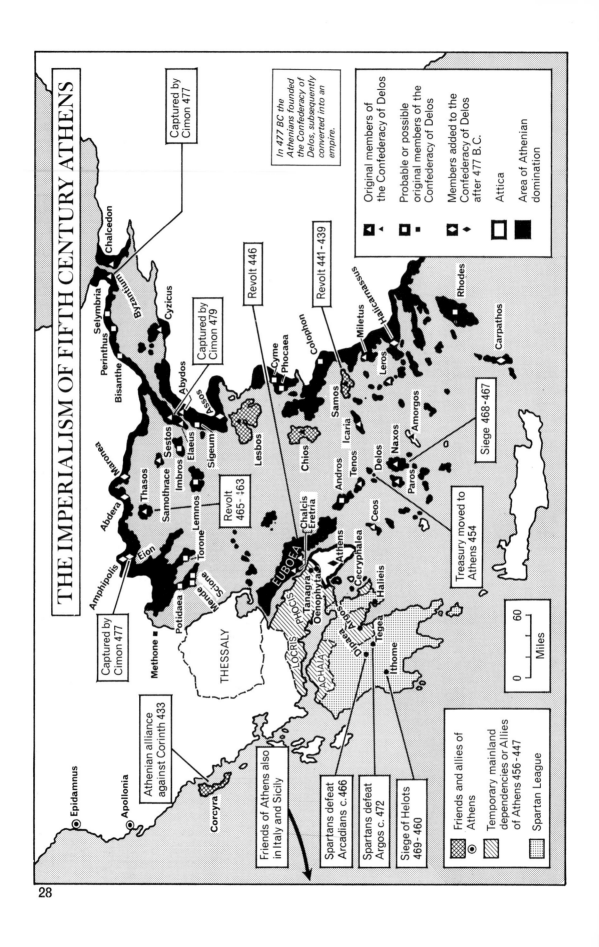

THE IMPERIALISM OF FIFTH CENTURY ATHENS

In 477 BC the Athenians founded the Confederacy of Delos, subsequently converted into an empire.

◄ Original members of the Confederacy of Delos

■ Probable or possible original members of the Confederacy of Delos

◆ Members added to the Confederacy of Delos after 477 B.C.

□ Attica

■ Area of Athenian domination

Captured by Cimon 477

Captured by Cimon 477

Captured by Cimon 479

Revolt 446

Revolt 441 - 439

Revolt 465 - 463

Siege 468 - 467

Treasury moved to Athens 454

Athenian alliance against Corinth 433

Friends of Athens also in Italy and Sicily

Spartans defeat Arcadians c. 466

Spartans defeat Argos c. 472

Siege of Helots 469 - 460

Epidamnus

Apollonia

Corcyra

Methone

Amphipolis

Eion

Abdera

Maroneia

Thasos

Samothrace

Imbros

Lemnos

Torone

Mende

Scione

Potidaea

Sestos

Elaeus

Sigeum

Assos

Abydos

Cyzicus

Byzantium

Chalcedon

Selymbria

Perinthus

Bisanthe

Lesbos

Chios

Cyme

Phocaea

Colophon

Miletus

Halicarnassus

Samos

Icaria

Leros

Rhodes

Carpathos

Andros

Tenos

Delos

Naxos

Amorgos

Paros

Ceos

Cecryphalea

THESSALY

LOCRIS

PHOCIS

Tanagra

Oenophyta

Chalcis

Eretria

EUBOEA

Athens

Megara

Aegina

ACHAIA

Tegea

Ithome

Halieis

Friends and allies of Athens

◉ Temporary mainland dependencies or Allies of Athens 456 - 447

Spartan League

Miles

0   60

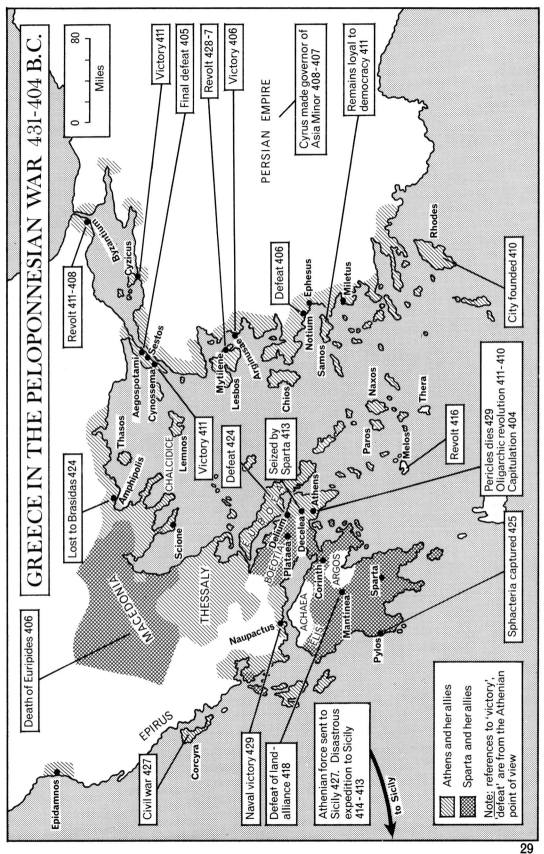

GREECE IN THE PELOPONNESIAN WAR 431–404 B.C.

0 ___ 80
Miles

Victory 411

Final defeat 405

Revolt 428-7

Victory 406

PERSIAN EMPIRE

Cyrus made governor of Asia Minor 408-407

Remains loyal to democracy 411

Revolt 411-408

Byzantium

Cyzicus

Rhodes

Defeat 406

Ephesus

Notium

Miletus

City founded 410

Aegospotami

Sestos

Cynossema

Mytilene

Lesbos

Arginusae

Samos

Chios

Thasos

Naxos

Paros

Thera

Victory 411

Defeat 424

Seized by Sparta 413

Amphipolis

CHALCIDICE

Lemnos

Scione

Melos

Revolt 416

Lost to Brasidas 424

Delium

EUBOEA

Athens

Decelea

BOEOTIA

Plataea

Corinth

ARGOS

Sparta

Mantinea

Pericles dies 429
Oligarchic revolution 411-410
Capitulation 404

Death of Euripides 406

THESSALY

ACHAEA

ELIS

Naupactus

Pylos

Sphacteria captured 425

MACEDONIA

Civil war 427

Corcyra

EPIRUS

Epidamnos

Naval victory 429

Defeat of land-alliance 418

Athenian force sent to Sicily 427. Disastrous expedition to Sicily 414–413

to Sicily

Athens and her allies

Sparta and her allies

Note: references to 'victory', 'defeat' are from the Athenian point of view

29

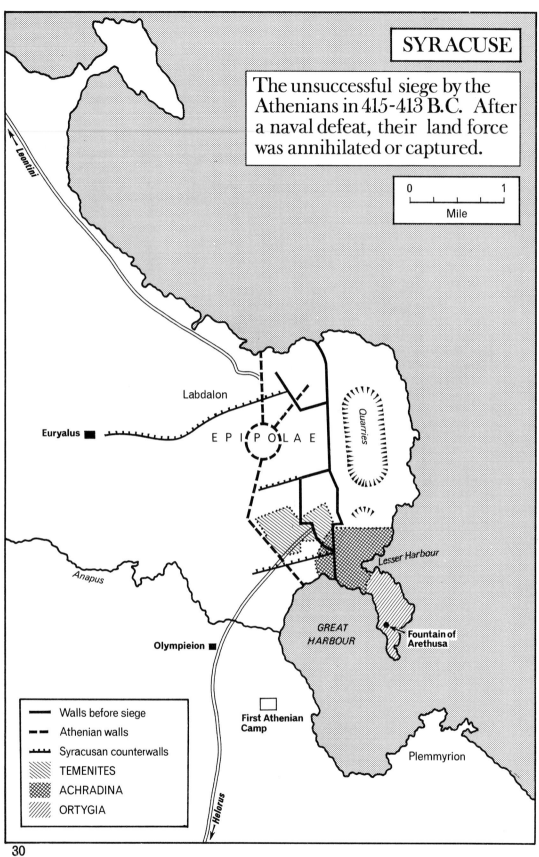

SYRACUSE

The unsuccessful siege by the Athenians in 415-413 B.C. After a naval defeat, their land force was annihilated or captured.

0   1
Mile

Leontini

Labdalon

Euryalus

E P I P O L A E

Quarries

Anapus

Lesser Harbour

GREAT
HARBOUR

Fountain of
Arethusa

Olympieion

First Athenian
Camp

Plemmyrion

— Walls before siege
-- Athenian walls
+++ Syracusan counterwalls
TEMENITES
ACHRADINA
ORTYGIA

Helorus

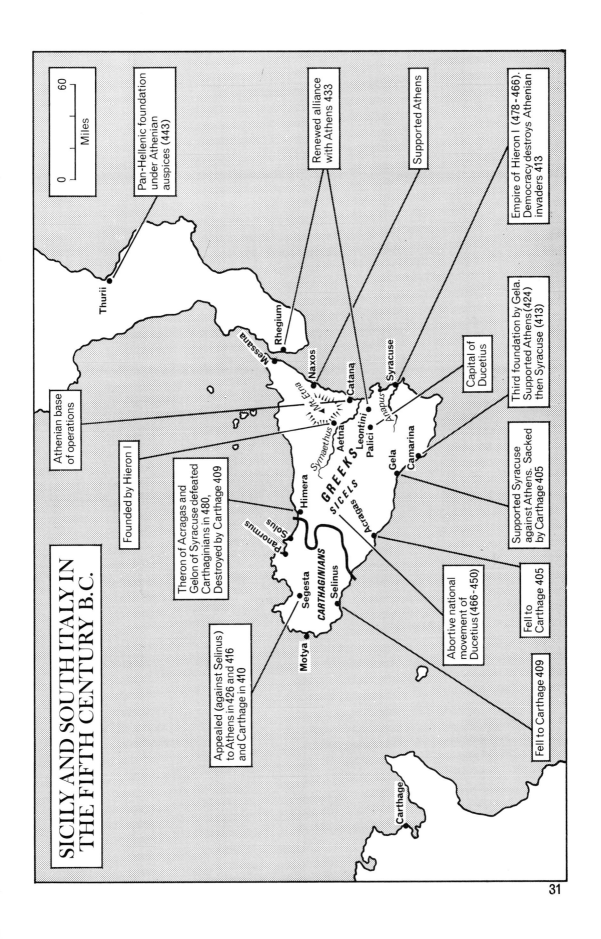

SICILY AND SOUTH ITALY IN THE FIFTH CENTURY B.C.

0 — 60 Miles

Thurii — Pan-Hellenic foundation under Athenian auspices (443)

Renewed alliance with Athens 433

Supported Athens

Empire of Hieron I (478–466). Democracy destroys Athenian invaders 413

Messana — Athenian base of operations

Rhegium

Naxos

Catana

Mt Etna

Aetna — Founded by Hieron I

Himera — Theron of Acragas and Gelon of Syracuse defeated Carthaginians in 480, Destroyed by Carthage 409

Symaethus

Leontini

Palici

GREEKS

SICELS

Anapus

Syracuse — Capital of Ducetius

Gela — Third foundation by Gela. Supported Athens (424) then Syracuse (413)

Camarina — Supported Syracuse against Athens. Sacked by Carthage 405

Acragas — Fell to Carthage 405

Panormus

Solus

CARTHAGINIANS

Segesta

Motya

Selinus — Appealed (against Selinus) to Athens in 426 and 416 and Carthage in 410

Abortive national movement of Ducetius (466–450)

Fell to Carthage 409

Carthage

31

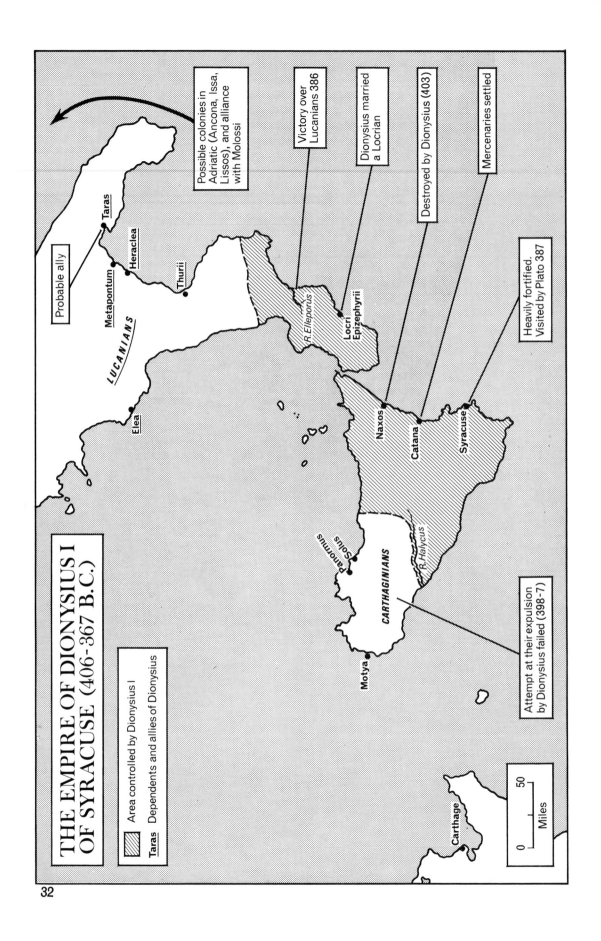

THE EMPIRE OF DIONYSIUS I
OF SYRACUSE (406-367 B.C.)

■ Area controlled by Dionysius I

▨ _Taras_ Dependents and allies of Dionysius

Possible colonies in Adriatic (Ancona, Issa, Lissos), and alliance with Molossi

Victory over Lucanians 386

Dionysius married a Locrian

Destroyed by Dionysius (403)

Mercenaries settled

Probable ally

Taras

Heraclea

Metapontum

Thurii

LUCANIANS

Elea

R. Eleporus

Locri Epizephyrii

Naxos

Catana

Syracuse

Heavily fortified. Visited by Plato 387

Panormus

Solus

CARTHAGINIANS

R. Halycus

Motya

Attempt at their expulsion by Dionysius failed (398-7)

Carthage

0   50

Miles

32

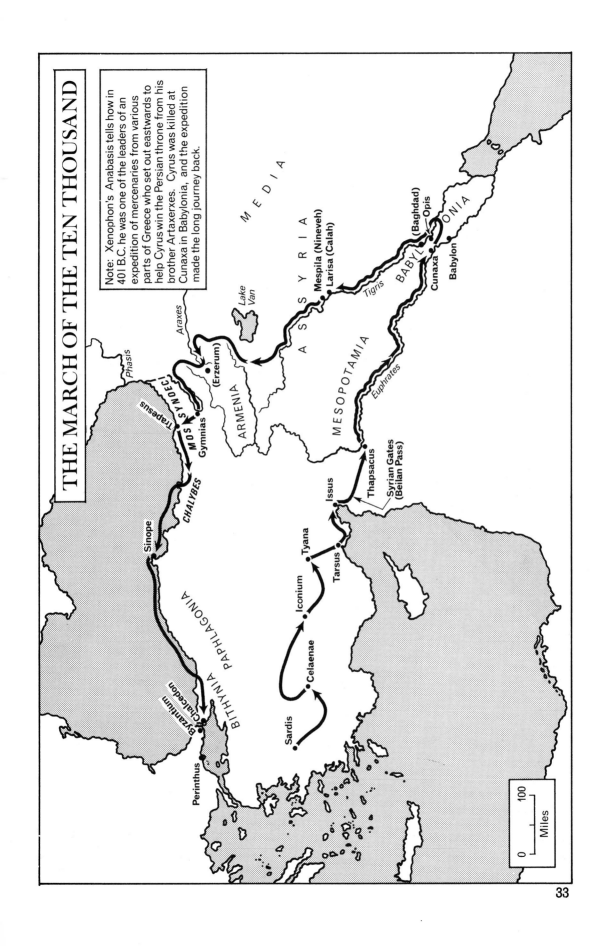

THE MARCH OF THE TEN THOUSAND

Note: Xenophon's Anabasis tells how in 401 B.C. he was one of the leaders of an expedition of mercenaries from various parts of Greece who set out eastwards to help Cyrus win the Persian throne from his brother Artaxerxes. Cyrus was killed at Cunaxa in Babylonia, and the expedition made the long journey back.

MEDIA

ASSYRIA

Mespila (Nineveh)
Larisa (Calah)

Tigris

BABYL (Baghdad)
Opis

ONIA

Cunaxa
Babylon

Lake Van

Araxes

(Erzerum)

ARMENIA

MESOPOTAMIA

Euphrates

Phasis

SYNOECI
MOS
Trapesus

Gymnias

CHALYBES

Thapsacus

Syrian Gates
(Beilan Pass)

Issus

Sinope

Tyana

Iconium

Tarsus

BITHYNIA PAPHLAGONIA

Celaenae

Sardis

Byzantium
Chalcedon

Perinthus

100

0

Miles

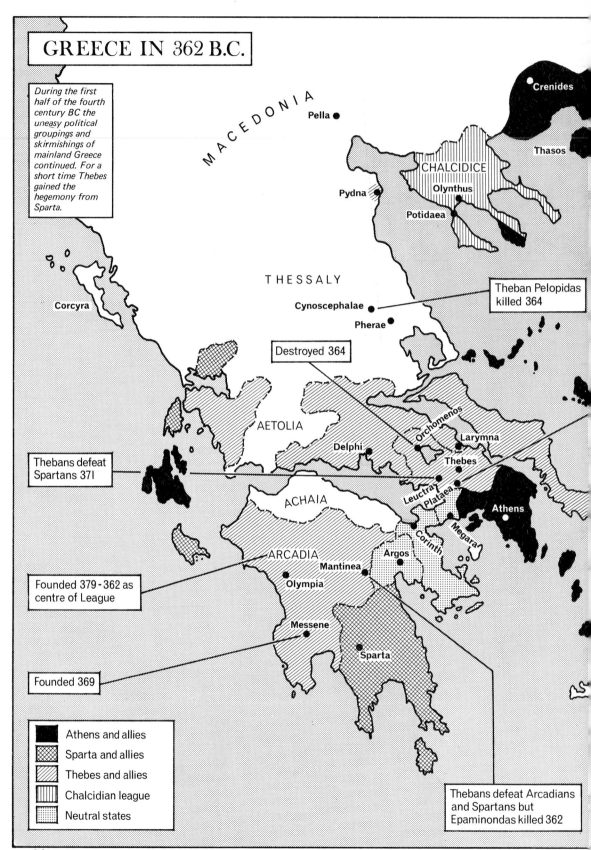

GREECE IN 362 B.C.

During the first half of the fourth century BC the uneasy political groupings and skirmishings of mainland Greece continued. For a short time Thebes gained the hegemony from Sparta.

MACEDONIA

Crenides

Pella

Thasos

CHALCIDICE

Olynthus

Pydna

Potidaea

THESSALY

Corcyra

Theban Pelopidas killed 364

Cynoscephalae

Pherae

Destroyed 364

AETOLIA

Orchomenos

Larymna

Delphi

Thebes

Thebans defeat Spartans 371

ACHAIA

Leuctra

Plataea

Athens

Megara

Corinth

ARCADIA

Argos

Mantinea

Founded 379-362 as centre of League

Olympia

Messene

Founded 369

Sparta

Athens and allies

Sparta and allies

Thebes and allies

Chalcidian league

Neutral states

Thebans defeat Arcadians and Spartans but Epaminondas killed 362

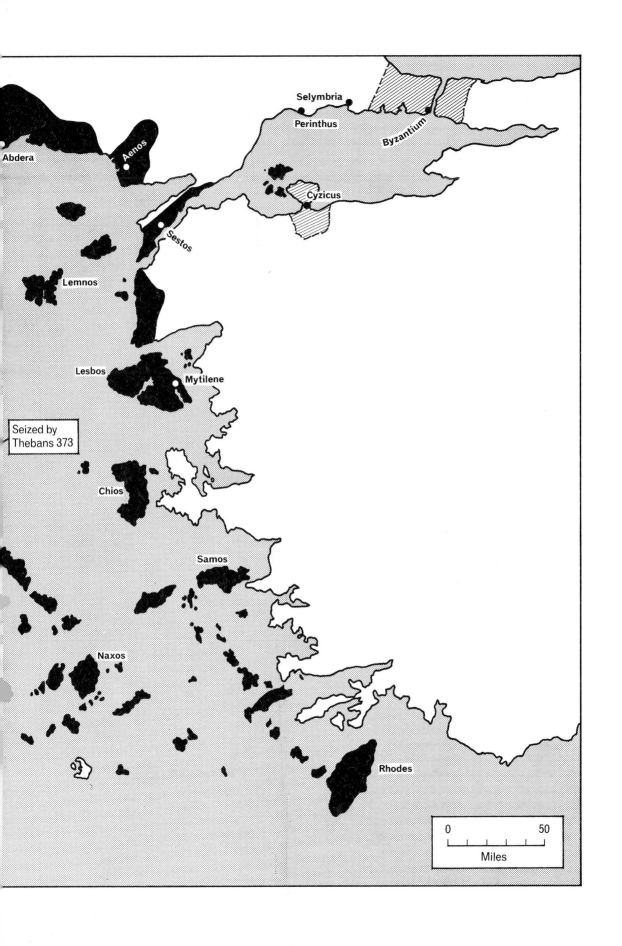

Selymbria

Perinthus

Byzantium

Abdera

Aenos

Sestos

Cyzicus

Lemnos

Lesbos

Mytilene

Seized by
Thebans 373

Chios

Samos

Naxos

Rhodes

0   50

Miles

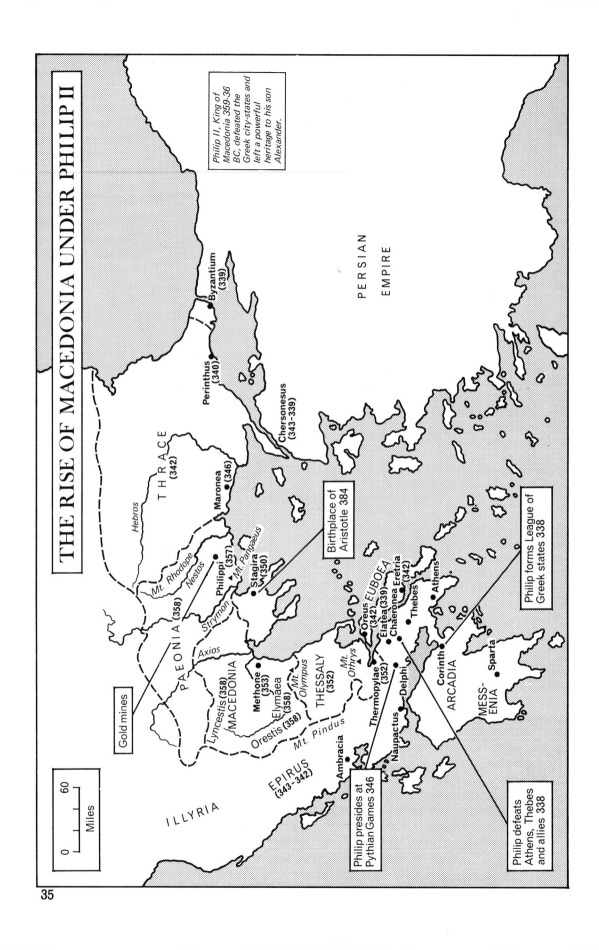

THE RISE OF MACEDONIA UNDER PHILIP II

Philip II, King of Macedonia 359-36 BC, defeated the Greek city-states and left a powerful heritage to his son Alexander.

PERSIAN EMPIRE

Byzantium (339)

Perinthus (340)

Chersonesus (343-339)

THRACE (342)

Maronea (346)

Hebros

Mt. Rhodope

Nestos

Philippi (357)

Mt. Pangaeus (350)

Stagira (358)

Birthplace of Aristotle 384

Gold mines

PAEONIA (358)

Strymon

Axios

Lyncestis (358)

MACEDONIA (358)

Methone (353)

Elymaea (358)

Orestis (358)

Mt. Olympus

Mt. Pindus

THESSALY (352)

Mt. Othrys

Oreus (342)

EUBOEA

Elatea (339)

Chaeronea

Eretria (342)

Thebes

Athens

Philip forms League of Greek states 338

Thermopylae (352)

Delphi

Corinth

ARCADIA

MESS-
ENIA

Sparta

Naupactus

Ambracia

EPIRUS (343-342)

ILLYRIA

Philip presides at Pythian Games 346

Philip defeats Athens, Thebes and allies 338

0   60
Miles

35

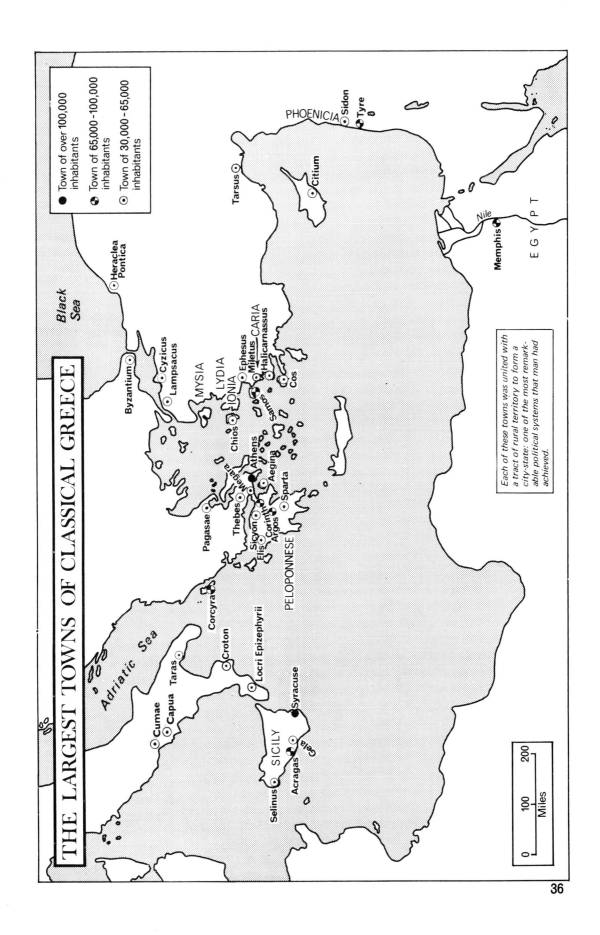

THE LARGEST TOWNS OF CLASSICAL GREECE

Town of over 100,000 inhabitants

Town of 65,000 - 100,000 inhabitants

Town of 30,000 - 65,000 inhabitants

Black Sea

PHOENICIA Sidon Tyre

Tarsus

Citium

Nile

Memphis E G Y P T

Heraclea Pontica

Cyzicus
Lampsacus

Byzantium

MYSIA

LYDIA

Ephesus
Miletus CARIA
Halicarnassus

Cos

IONIA

Chios Samos

Athens

Megara Aegina

Sparta

Pagasae

Thebes

Sicyon Corinth
Elis Argos

PELOPONNESE

Corcyra

Croton

Locri Epizephyrii

Taras

Adriatic Sea

Cumae Capua

Syracuse

SICILY Gela

Selinus Acragas

Each of these towns was united with a tract of rural territory to form a city-state: one of the most remarkable political systems that man had achieved.

0 100 200
Miles

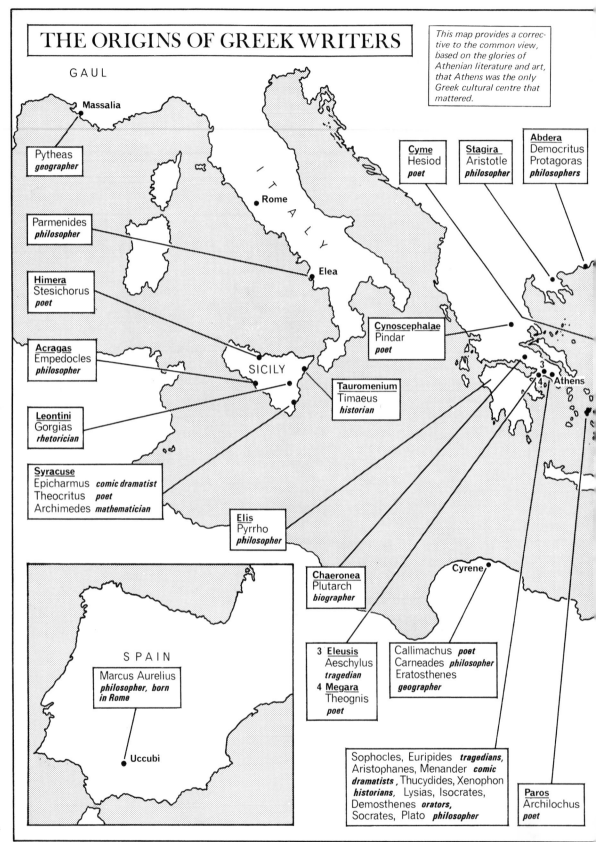

THE ORIGINS OF GREEK WRITERS

GAUL

This map provides a corrective to the common view, based on the glories of Athenian literature and art, that Athens was the only Greek cultural centre that mattered.

Massalia

Pytheas
geographer

Rome

I T A L Y

Parmenides
philosopher

Elea

Himera
Stesichorus
poet

Acragas
Empedocles
philosopher

SICILY

Leontini
Gorgias
rhetorician

Syracuse
Epicharmus   *comic dramatist*
Theocritus   *poet*
Archimedes   *mathematician*

Elis
Pyrrho
philosopher

Cyme
Hesiod
poet

Stagira
Aristotle
philosopher

Abdera
Democritus
Protagoras
philosophers

Cynoscephalae
Pindar
poet

Tauromenium
Timaeus
historian

3
4   Athens

Chaeronea
Plutarch
biographer

Cyrene

SPAIN

Marcus Aurelius
philosopher, born in Rome

Uccubi

3 **Eleusis**
  Aeschylus
  tragedian
4 **Megara**
  Theognis
  poet

Callimachus   *poet*
Carneades   *philosopher*
Eratosthenes
geographer

Sophocles, Euripides *tragedians*,
Aristophanes, Menander *comic
dramatists*, Thucydides, Xenophon
historians, Lysias, Isocrates,
Demosthenes *orators*,
Socrates, Plato *philosopher*

Paros
Archilochus
poet

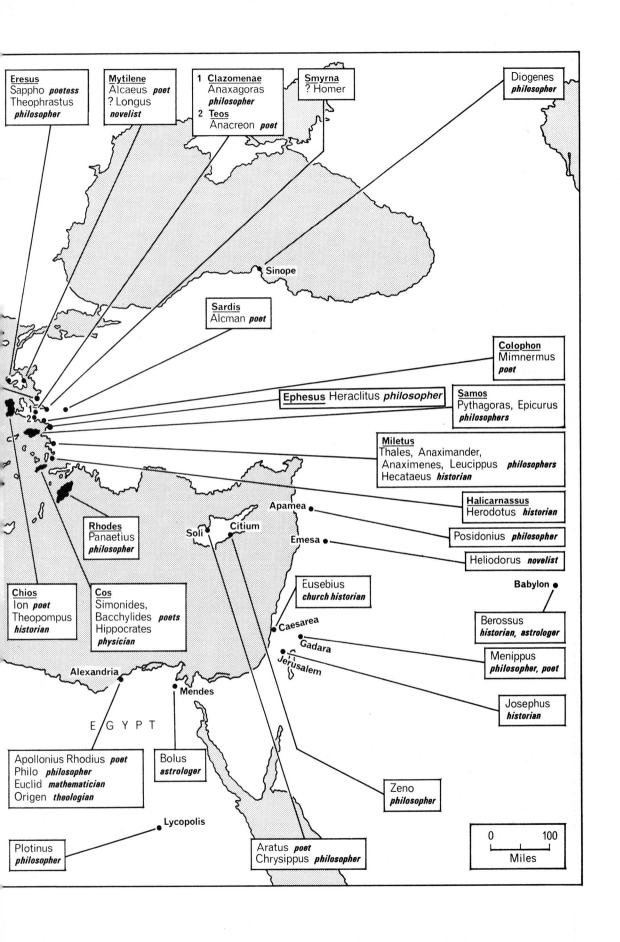

Eresus
Sappho *poetess*
Theophrastus *philosopher*

Mytilene
Alcaeus *poet*
? Longus *novelist*

1 **Clazomenae**
Anaxagoras *philosopher*
2 **Teos**
Anacreon *poet*

Smyrna
? Homer

Diogenes *philosopher*

Sinope

Sardis
Alcman *poet*

Colophon
Mimnermus *poet*

Ephesus Heraclitus *philosopher*

Samos
Pythagoras, Epicurus *philosophers*

Miletus
Thales, Anaximander, Anaximenes, Leucippus *philosophers*
Hecataeus *historian*

Apamea

Halicarnassus
Herodotus *historian*

Rhodes
Panaetius *philosopher*

Soli

Citium

Emesa

Posidonius *philosopher*

Heliodorus *novelist*

Chios
Ion *poet*
Theopompus *historian*

Cos
Simonides, Bacchylides *poets*
Hippocrates *physician*

Eusebius *church historian*

Babylon

Berossus *historian, astrologer*

Caesarea

Gadara

Jerusalem

Menippus *philosopher, poet*

Alexandria

Mendes

Josephus *historian*

E G Y P T

Apollonius Rhodius *poet*
Philo *philosopher*
Euclid *mathematician*
Origen *theologian*

Bolus *astrologer*

Zeno *philosopher*

Lycopolis

Plotinus *philosopher*

Aratus *poet*
Chrysippus *philosopher*

0   100
Miles

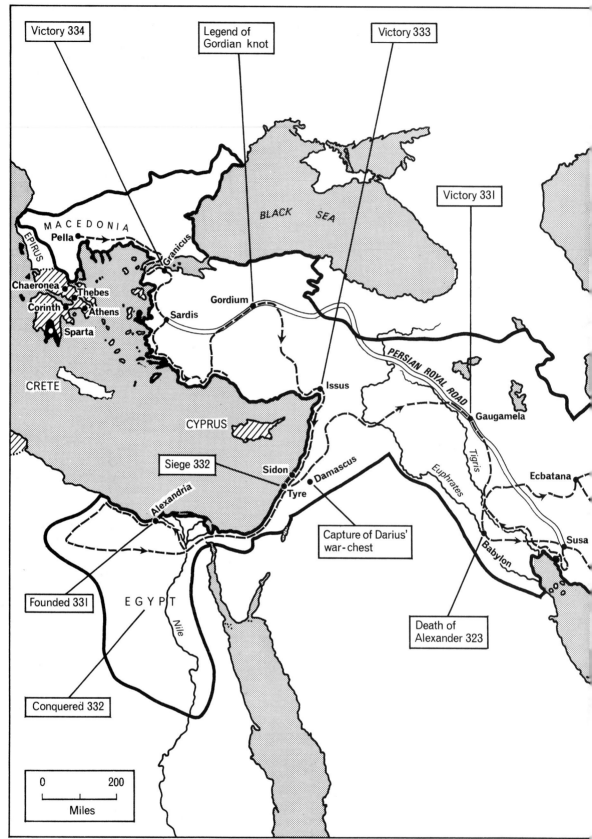

Victory 334

Legend of Gordian knot

Victory 333

Victory 331

BLACK SEA

MACEDONIA

EPIRUS

Pella

Chaeronea

Corinth

Thebes

Athens

Sparta

CRETE

Granicus

Sardis

Gordium

CYPRUS

Issus

PERSIAN ROYAL ROAD

Gaugamela

Ecbatana

Tigris

Euphrates

Siege 332

Sidon

Damascus

Tyre

Capture of Darius' war-chest

Babylon

Susa

Alexandria

Founded 331

EGYPT

Nile

Death of Alexander 323

Conquered 332

0   200

Miles

THE CONQUESTS OF ALEXANDER THE GREAT

Alexander III of Macedonia succeeded his father Philip II in 336, and, after conquests that utterly changed the world, died at Babylon in 323.

☐ Empire of Alexander the Great
▨ Dependent states
■ Independent states
– – –▶ Routes of Alexander the Great

Conquered 328

Darius murdered 330

CASPIAN SEA

SOGDIANA

Alexandria Eschate

PUNJAB

Alexandria (Merv)

Bactra (Balkh)

BACTRIA

Alexandria

Damghan

PARTHIA

Alexandria (Herat)

Alexandria (Ghazni)

Taxila

Indus

Hydaspes

Bucephala

Occupied 331

Persepolis

Alexandria (Kandahar)

Alexandria

PERSIAN GULF

GEDROSIA

Victory over Indian king Porus 326

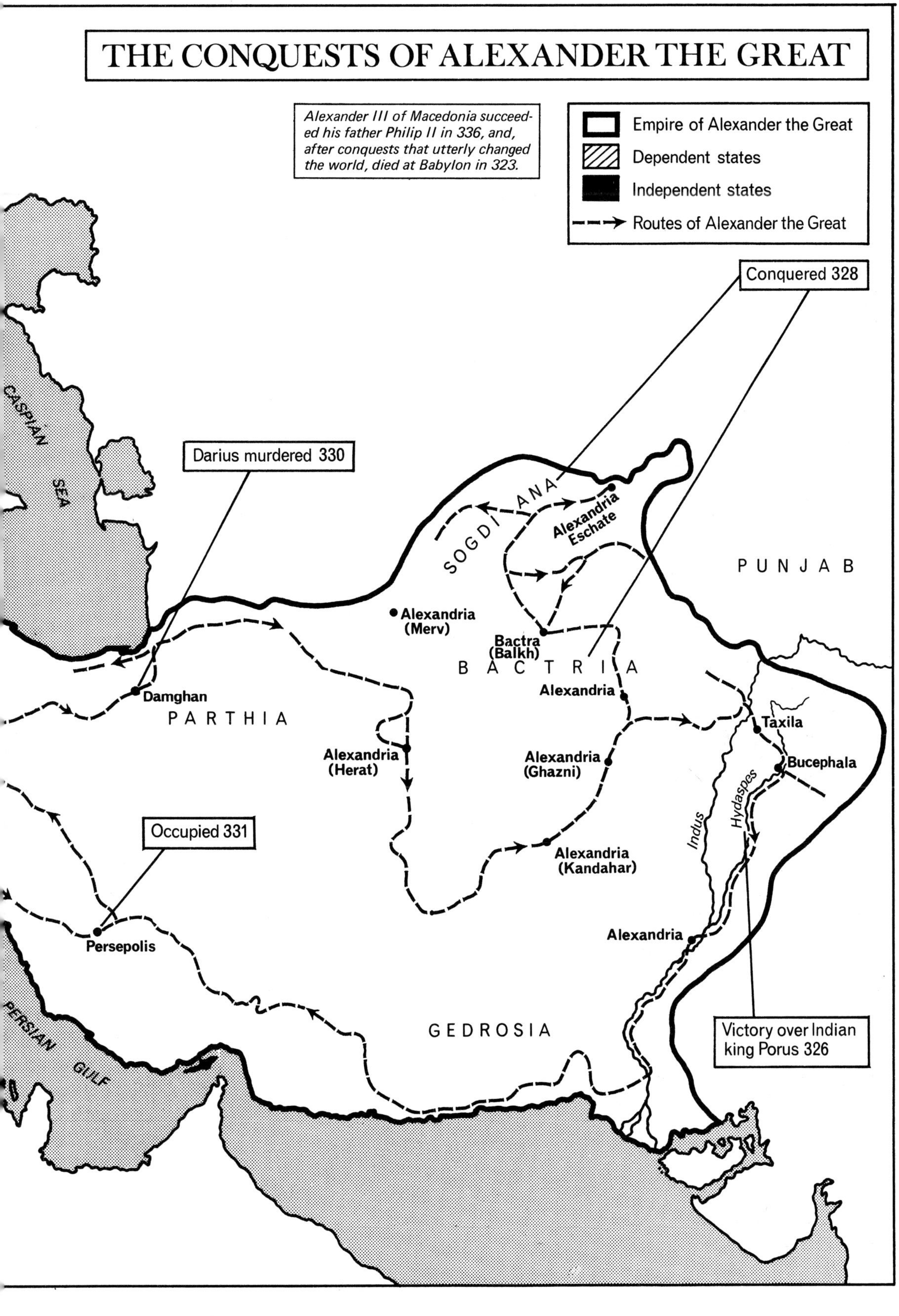

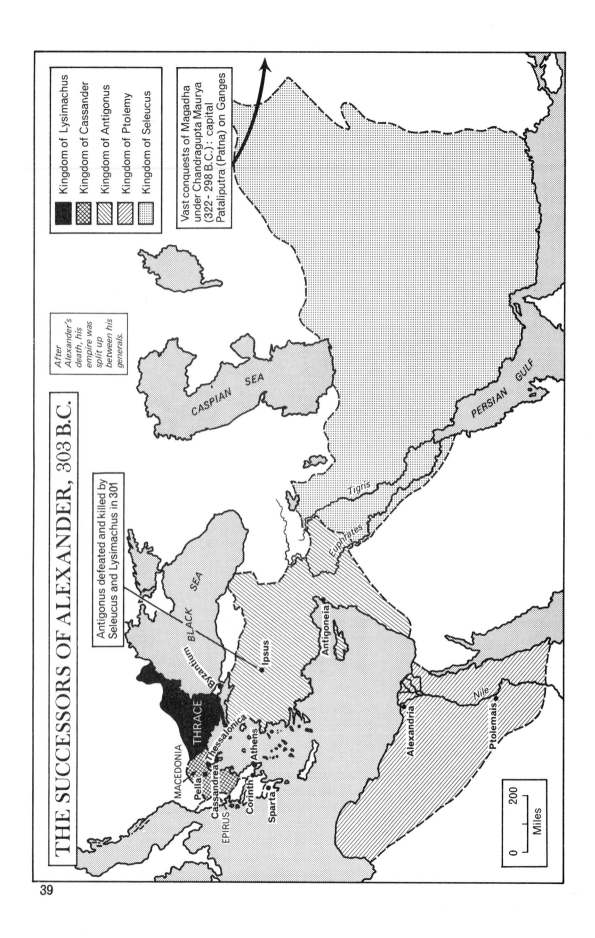

THE SUCCESSORS OF ALEXANDER, 303 B.C.

Kingdom of Lysimachus
Kingdom of Cassander
Kingdom of Antigonus
Kingdom of Ptolemy
Kingdom of Seleucus

Vast conquests of Magadha under Chandragupta Maurya (322 - 298 B.C.): capital Pataliputra (Patna) on Ganges

After Alexander's death, his empire was split up between his generals.

Antigonus defeated and killed by Seleucus and Lysimachus in 301

CASPIAN SEA

PERSIAN GULF

Tigris

Euphrates

BLACK SEA

Byzantium

Ipsus

Antigoneia

Nile

MACEDONIA

THRACE

Pella

Cassandrea

Thessalonica

EPIRUS

Corinth

Athens

Sparta

Alexandria

Ptolemais

0   200

Miles

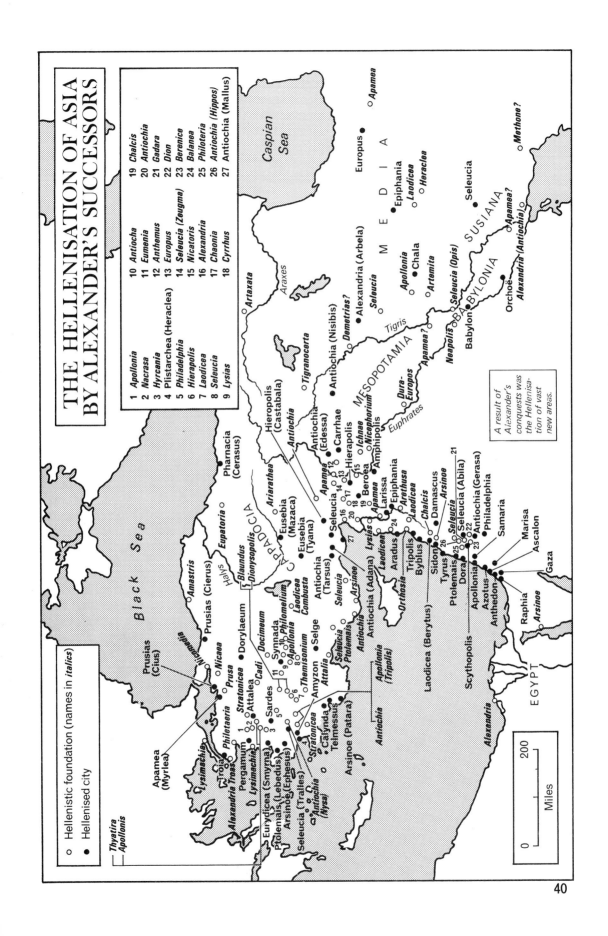

THE HELLENISATION OF ASIA
BY ALEXANDER'S SUCCESSORS

1 *Apollonia*	10 *Antiocha*	19 *Chalcis*	
2 *Nacrasa*	11 *Eumenia*	20 *Antiochia*	
3 *Hyrcania*	12 *Anthemus*	21 *Gadara*	
4 *Plistarchea (Heraclea)*	13 *Europus*	22 *Dion*	
5 *Philadelphia*	14 *Seleucia (Zeugma)*	23 *Berenice*	
6 *Hierapolis*	15 *Nicatoris*	24 *Balanea*	
7 *Laodicea*	16 *Alexandria*	25 *Philoteria*	
8 *Seleucia*	17 *Chaonia*	26 *Antiochia (Hippos)*	
9 *Lysias*	18 *Cyrrhus*	27 *Antiochia (Mallus)*	

○ Hellenistic foundation (names in *italics*)
● Hellenised city

Thyatira
Apollonis

A result of Alexander's conquests was the Hellenisation of vast new areas.

0   200
Miles

Caspian Sea

Black Sea

40

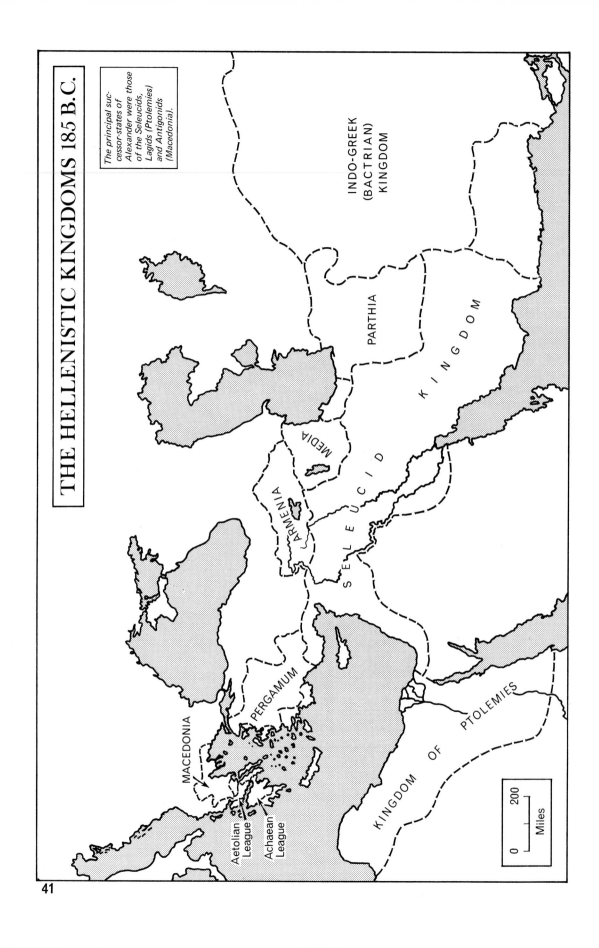

THE HELLENISTIC KINGDOMS 185 B.C.

The principal successor-states of Alexander were those of the Seleucids, Lagids (Ptolemies) and Antigonids (Macedonia).

INDO-GREEK
(BACTRIAN)
KINGDOM

PARTHIA

S E L E U C I D

K I N G D O M

MEDIA

ARMENIA

MACEDONIA

PERGAMUM

Aetolian
League

Achaean
League

KINGDOM OF PTOLEMIES

0 200
Miles

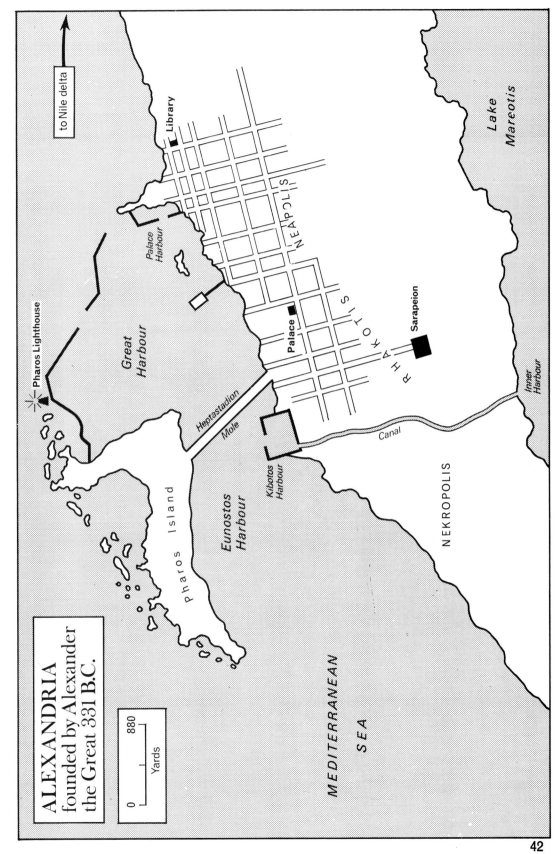

ALEXANDRIA
founded by Alexander
the Great 331 B.C.

0   880
Yards

to Nile delta

Library

Palace

Sarapeion

NEAPOLIS

RHAKOTIS

Palace Harbour

Great Harbour

Pharos Lighthouse

Heptastadion Mole

Pharos Island

Eunostos Harbour

Kibotos Harbour

Canal

Inner Harbour

Lake Mareotis

NEKROPOLIS

MEDITERRANEAN SEA

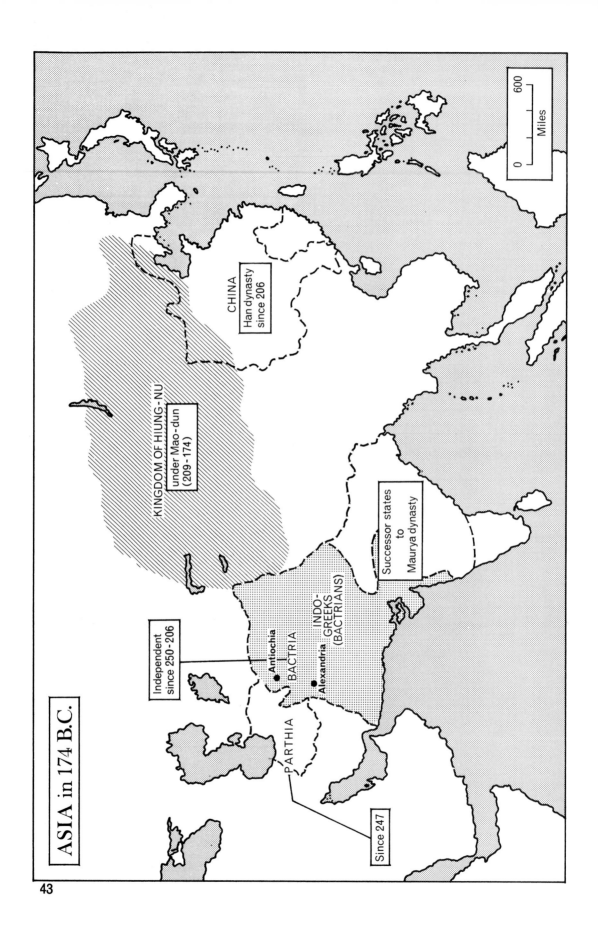

ASIA in 174 B.C.

KINGDOM OF HIUNG-NU
under Mao-dun
(209-174)

CHINA
Han dynasty
since 206

Successor states
to
Maurya dynasty

Independent
since 250-206

Antiochia
BACTRIA
Alexandria

INDO-
GREEKS
(BACTRIANS)

PARTHIA

Since 247

600
Miles
0

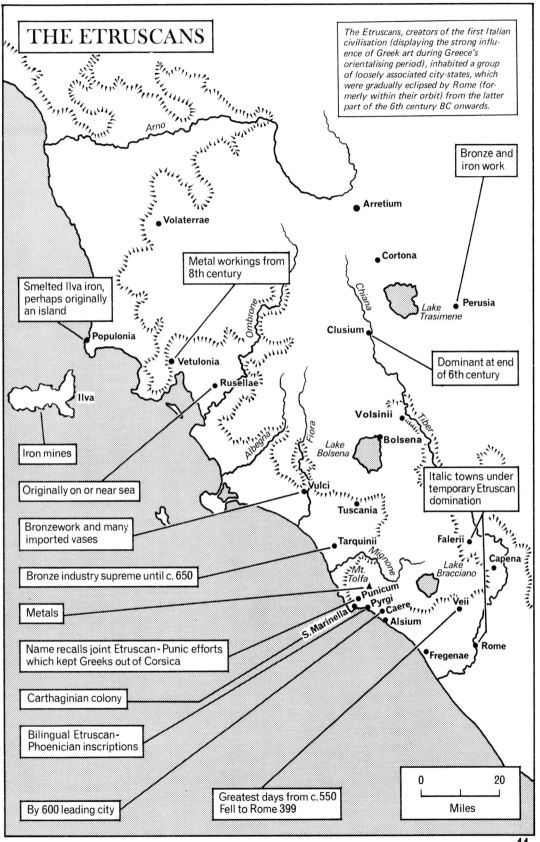

THE ETRUSCANS

The Etruscans, creators of the first Italian civilisation (displaying the strong influence of Greek art during Greece's orientalising period), inhabited a group of loosely associated city-states, which were gradually eclipsed by Rome (formerly within their orbit) from the latter part of the 6th century BC onwards.

Arno

Bronze and iron work

• **Arretium**

• **Volaterrae**

• **Cortona**

Chiana

Metal workings from 8th century

Smelted Ilva iron, perhaps originally an island

• **Perusia**

Lake Trasimene

• **Clusium**

Dominant at end of 6th century

• **Populonia**

Ombrone

• **Vetulonia**

Ilva

• **Rusellae**

Volsinii

Tiber

• **Bolsena**

Iron mines

Fiora

Lake Bolsena

Albegna

Originally on or near sea

Italic towns under temporary Etruscan domination

Bronzework and many imported vases

• **Vulci**

• **Tuscania**

Falerii

Lake Bracciano

Capena

Bronze industry supreme until c. 650

• **Tarquinii**

Mignone

Mt. Tolfa

Metals

• **Punicum**
• **Pyrgi**
• **Caere**

• **Veii**

Name recalls joint Etruscan-Punic efforts which kept Greeks out of Corsica

S. Marinella

• **Alsium**

Rome

Carthaginian colony

• **Fregenae**

Bilingual Etruscan-Phoenician inscriptions

0   20

Miles

By 600 leading city

Greatest days from c. 550
Fell to Rome 399

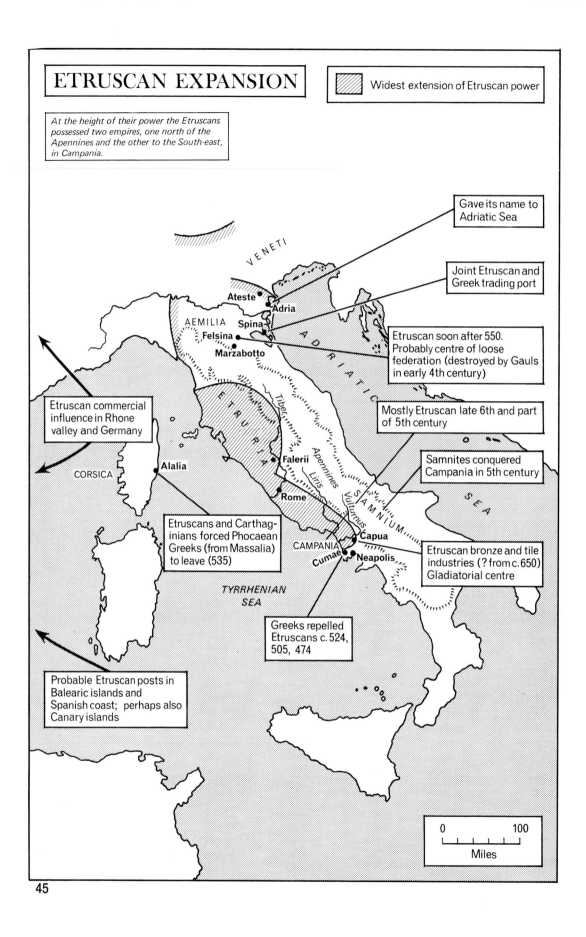

ETRUSCAN EXPANSION

Widest extension of Etruscan power

At the height of their power the Etruscans possessed two empires, one north of the Apennines and the other to the South-east, in Campania.

VENETI

Ateste ● ● Adria

AEMILIA Spina

● Felsina

Marzabotto

ADRIATIC

ETRURIA

Tiber

Falerii

Apennines

Liris

Rome

Vulturnus

SAMNIUM

SEA

CORSICA

● Alalia

CAMPANIA Capua

Cumae ● ● Neapolis

Gave its name to Adriatic Sea

Joint Etruscan and Greek trading port

Etruscan soon after 550. Probably centre of loose federation (destroyed by Gauls in early 4th century)

Mostly Etruscan late 6th and part of 5th century

Samnites conquered Campania in 5th century

Etruscan commercial influence in Rhone valley and Germany

Etruscans and Carthaginians forced Phocaean Greeks (from Massalia) to leave (535)

Etruscan bronze and tile industries (? from c.650) Gladiatorial centre

TYRRHENIAN SEA

Greeks repelled Etruscans c. 524, 505, 474

Probable Etruscan posts in Balearic islands and Spanish coast; perhaps also Canary islands

0   100

Miles

45

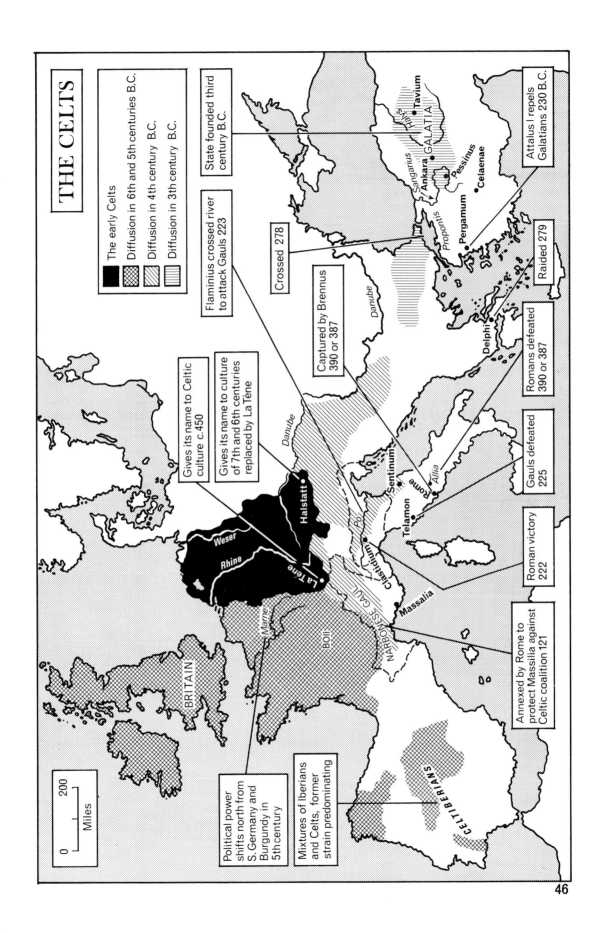

THE CELTS

The early Celts

Diffusion in 6th and 5th centuries B.C.

Diffusion in 4th century B.C.

Diffusion in 3rd century B.C.

State founded third century B.C.

Flaminius crossed river to attack Gauls 223

Crossed 278

Captured by Brennus 390 or 387

Gives its name to Celtic culture c.450

Gives its name to culture of 7th and 6th centuries replaced by La Tène

Political power shifts north from S. Germany and Burgundy in 5th century

Mixtures of Iberians and Celts, former strain predominating

Annexed by Rome to protect Massilia against Celtic coalition 121

Roman victory 222

Gauls defeated 225

Romans defeated 390 or 387

Raided 279

Attalus I repels Galatians 230 B.C.

GALATIA

Tavium

Ankara

Pessinus

Celaenae

Pergamum

Sangarius

Propontis

Delphi

Rome

Allia

Sentinum

Telamon

Mediolanum

Massalia

Po

La Tène

Halstatt

Weser

Rhine

Danube

Danube

Marne

BRITAIN

BOII

NARBONESE GAUL

CISALPINE GAUL

CELTIBERIANS

0   200
Miles

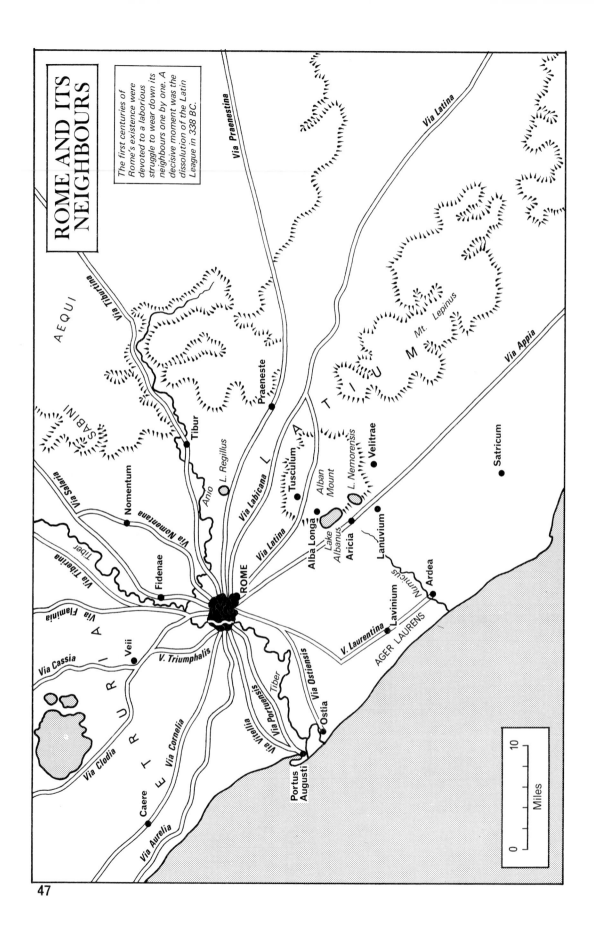

ROME AND ITS NEIGHBOURS

The first centuries of Rome's existence were devoted to a laborious struggle to wear down its neighbours one by one. A decisive moment was the dissolution of the Latin League in 338 BC.

Via Latina

Via Praenestina

Via Appia

Mt. Lepinus

AEQUI

Via Tiburtina

SABINI

Via Salaria

Tibur

L. Regillus

Anio

Praeneste

Via Labicana

L A T I U M

Tusculum

Velitrae

Via Latina

Alban Mount

L. Nemorensis

Nomentum

Via Nomentana

Alba Longa

Lake Albanus

Aricia

Satricum

Lanuvium

Fidenae

Tiber

Via Tiburtina

Via Flaminia

ROME

Via Latina

Lavinium

Numicius

Ardea

Veii

V. Triumphalis

AGER LAURENS

V. Laurentina

Via Cassia

E T R U R I A

Tiber

Via Ostiensis

Via Viae

Via Portuensis

Ostia

Via Clodia

Via Cornelia

Portus Augusti

Caere

Via Aurelia

0   10

Miles

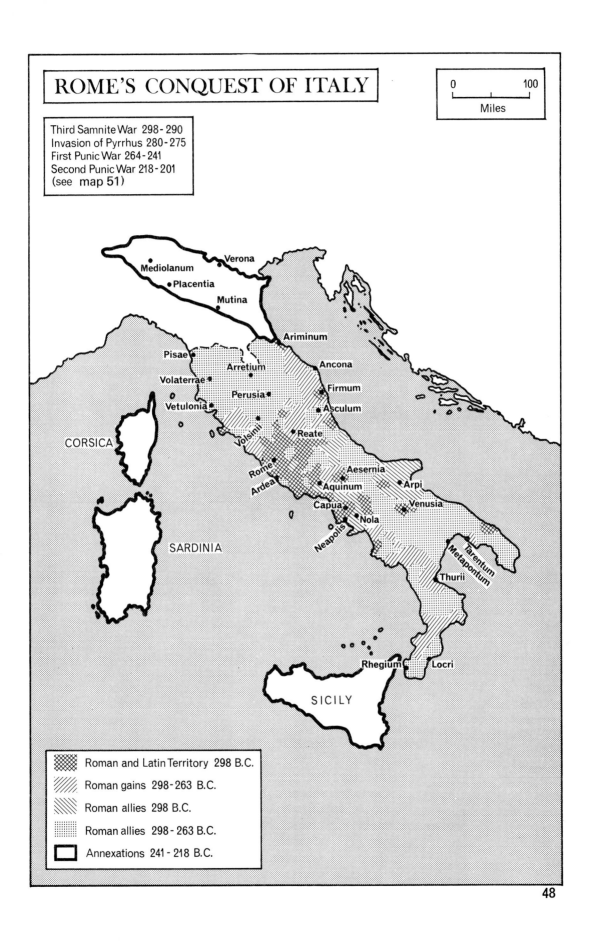

ROME'S CONQUEST OF ITALY

0   100

Miles

Third Samnite War 298-290
Invasion of Pyrrhus 280-275
First Punic War 264-241
Second Punic War 218-201
(see **map 51**)

Verona

Mediolanum

Placentia

Mutina

Ariminum

Pisae

Arretium

Ancona

Volaterrae

Firmum

Perusia

Vetulonia

Asculum

Volsinii

Reate

CORSICA

Rome

Aesernia

Ardea

Arpi

Aquinum

Venusia

Capua

Nola

Neapolis

SARDINIA

Tarentum

Metapontum

Thurii

Rhegium

Locri

SICILY

Roman and Latin Territory 298 B.C.

Roman gains 298-263 B.C.

Roman allies 298 B.C.

Roman allies 298-263 B.C.

Annexations 241-218 B.C.

48

THE ROADS OF ROMAN ITALY

0   100
Miles

Augusta Praetoria

Mediolanum

Segusio

Dertona

Genua ⑥

⑧

Luna

Pisae

Vada Volaterrana

CORSICA

Placentia

Cremona

Verona ⑥

①

Mantua

Po

Ravenna

Ariminum

Florentia

Fanum Fortunae

Arretium

ADRIATIC

Truentum

Reate

Aternum

Tibur

Corfinium

Anagnia

Fregellae

Capua

Canusium

Beneventum ⑩

Venusia ②

Brundisium

Tarentum

SARDINIA

TYRRHENIAN SEA

Rhegium

SICILY

Aquileia

①

⑥

①

③

⑪

④

⑬

⑦

ROME

②

⑤

Tarracina

Cales

Casilinum

Neapolis

⑫

⑨

SEA

① Via Aemilia (187 B.C.)
② Via Appia (312 - 244 B.C.)
③ Via Aurelia
④ Via Flaminia (220 B.C.)
⑤ Via Latina
⑥ Via Postumia (148 B.C.)
⑦ Via Valeria

⑧ Via Julia Augusta
⑨ Via Domitiana
⑩ Via Trajana
⑪ Via Cassia
⑫ Via Popillia
⑬ Via Salaria

49

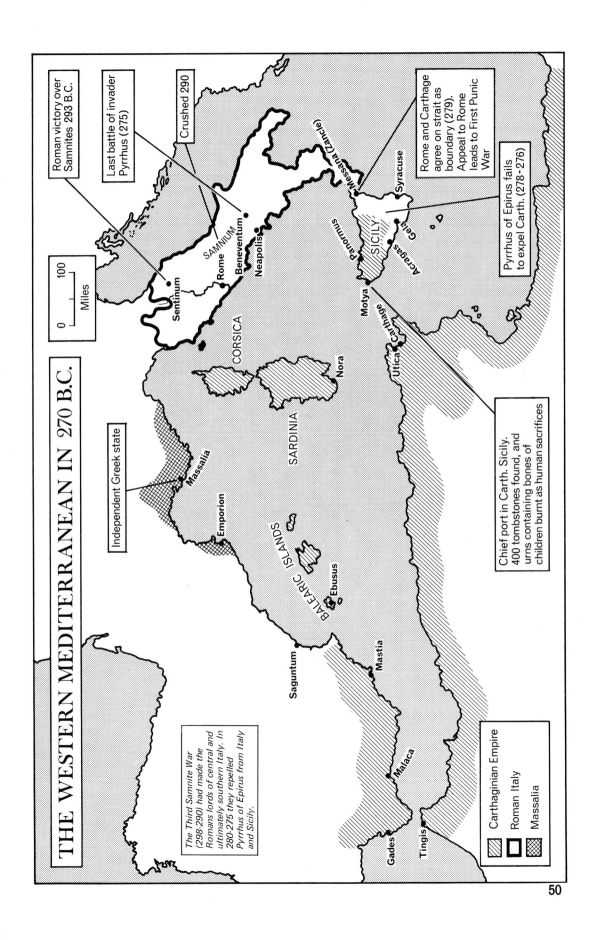

THE WESTERN MEDITERRANEAN IN 270 B.C.

Roman victory over Samnites 293 B.C.

Last battle of invader Pyrrhus (275)

Crushed 290

Rome and Carthage agree on strait as boundary (279). Appeal to Rome leads to First Punic War

Pyrrhus of Epirus fails to expel Carth. (278 - 276)

Chief port in Carth. Sicily. 400 tombstones found, and urns containing bones of children burnt as human sacrifices

Independent Greek state

100

0

Miles

The Third Samnite War (298-290) had made the Romans lords of central and ultimately southern Italy. In 280-275 they repelled Pyrrhus of Epirus from Italy and Sicily.

SAMNIUM

Rome

Sentinum

Beneventum

Neapolis

Messana (Zancle)

Panormus

Syracuse

SICILY

Gela

Acragas

Motya

Utica

Carthage

CORSICA

Nora

SARDINIA

Massalia

Emporion

BALEARIC ISLANDS

Ebusus

Saguntum

Mastia

Malaca

Tingis

Gades

Carthaginian Empire

Roman Italy

Massalia

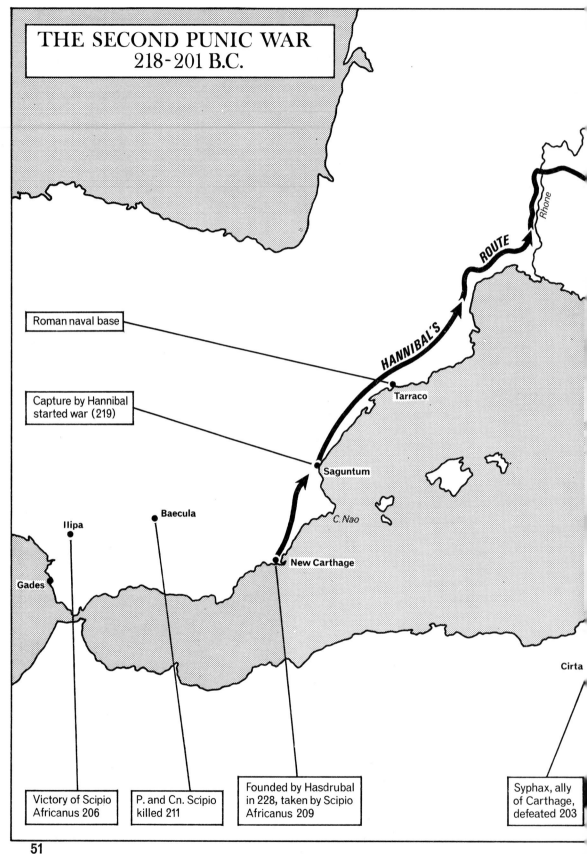

THE SECOND PUNIC WAR
218-201 B.C.

Rhone

HANNIBAL'S ROUTE

Roman naval base

Capture by Hannibal started war (219)

Tarraco

Saguntum

Baecula

Ilipa

C. Nao

New Carthage

Gades

Cirta

Victory of Scipio Africanus 206

P. and Cn. Scipio killed 211

Founded by Hasdrubal in 228, taken by Scipio Africanus 209

Syphax, ally of Carthage, defeated 203

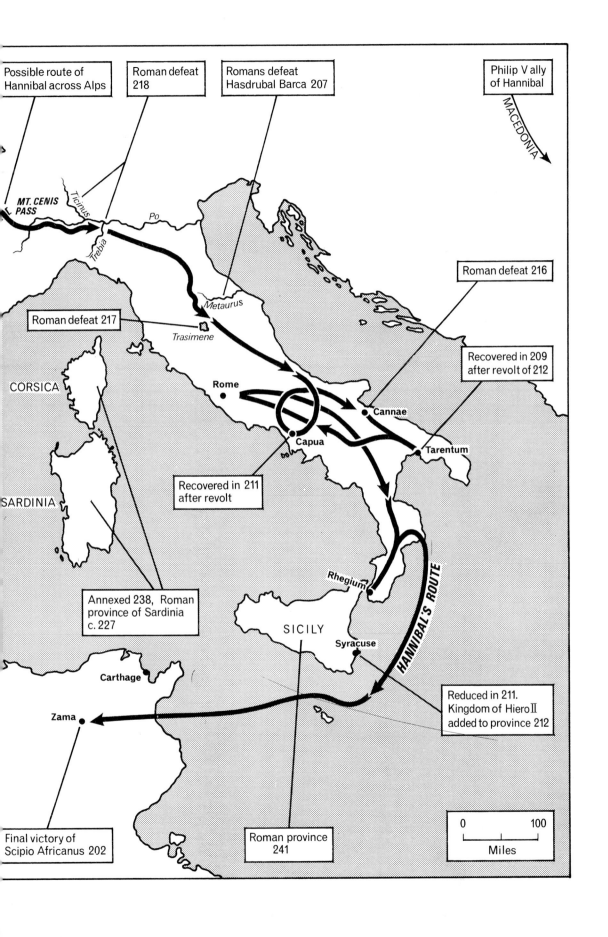

Possible route of
Hannibal across Alps

Roman defeat
218

Romans defeat
Hasdrubal Barca 207

Philip V ally
of Hannibal

MACEDONIA

MT. CENIS
PASS

Ticinus

Po

Trebia

Metaurus

Roman defeat 217

Trasimene

Roman defeat 216

CORSICA

Rome

Recovered in 209
after revolt of 212

Cannae

Capua

Tarentum

SARDINIA

Recovered in 211
after revolt

Annexed 238, Roman
province of Sardinia
c. 227

Rhegium

HANNIBAL'S ROUTE

SICILY

Syracuse

Carthage

Reduced in 211.
Kingdom of Hiero II
added to province 212

Zama

Final victory of
Scipio Africanus 202

Roman province
241

0   100

Miles

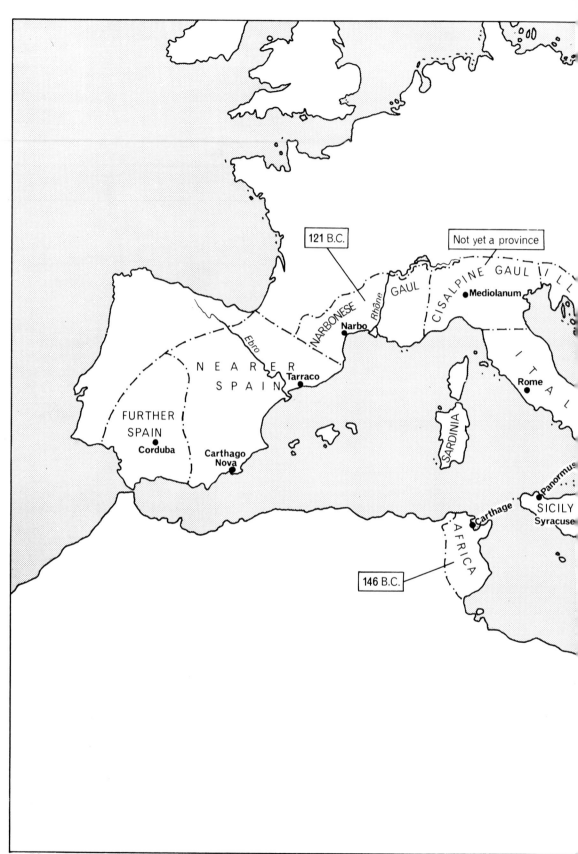

121 B.C.

Not yet a province

GAUL

CISALPINE GAUL

Mediolanum

NARBONESE

Rhône

Narbo

NEARER
SPAIN

Tarraco

Rome

ITALY

SARDINIA

FURTHER
SPAIN

Corduba

Carthago
Nova

Panormus

SICILY

Syracuse

Carthage

AFRICA

146 B.C.

Ebro

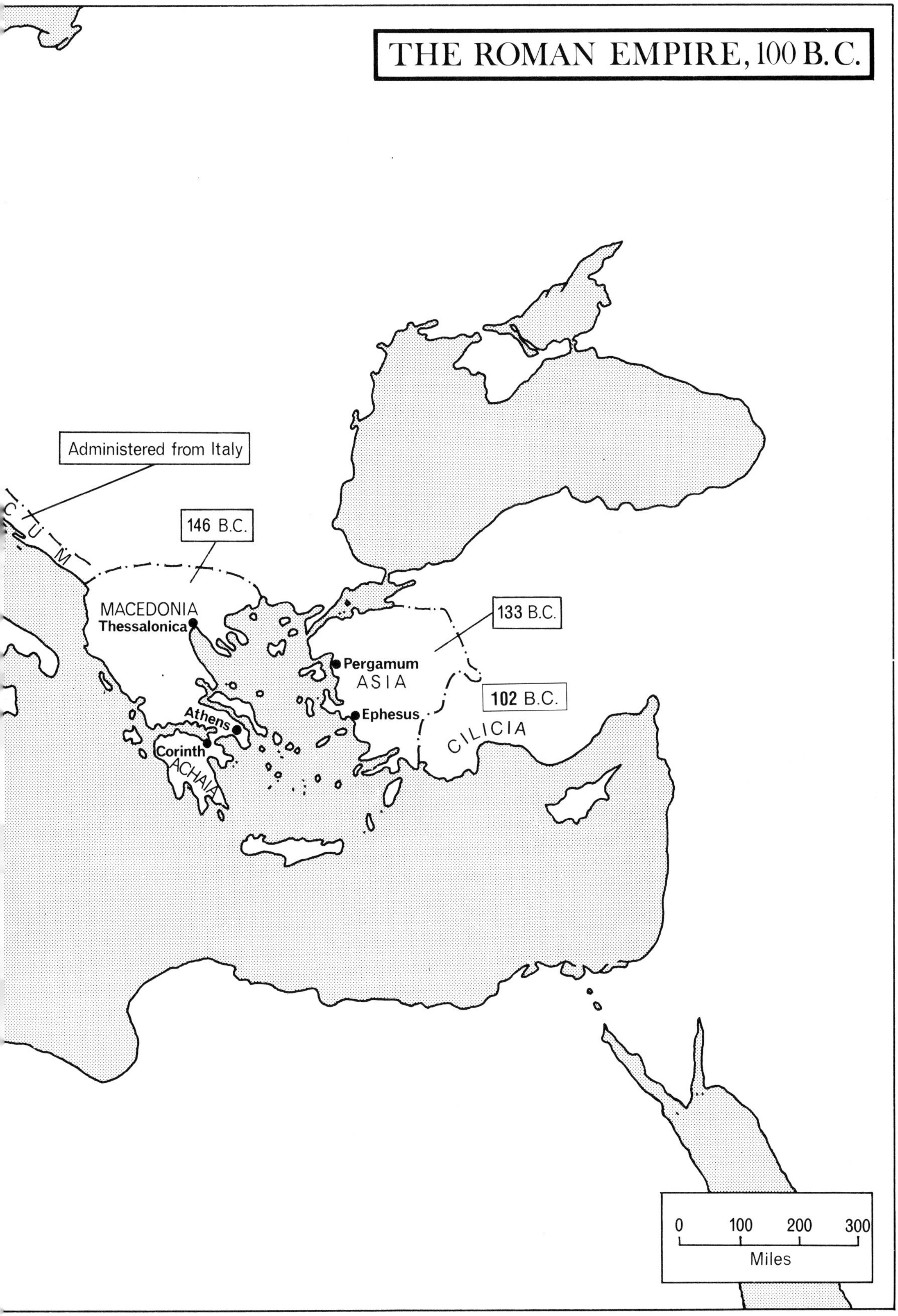

THE ROMAN EMPIRE, 100 B.C.

Administered from Italy

146 B.C.

133 B.C.

102 B.C.

T Y R R H E N U M

MACEDONIA
Thessalonica

Pergamum
ASIA

Athens

CILICIA

Corinth
ACHAIA

Ephesus

| 0 | 100 | 200 | 300 |

Miles

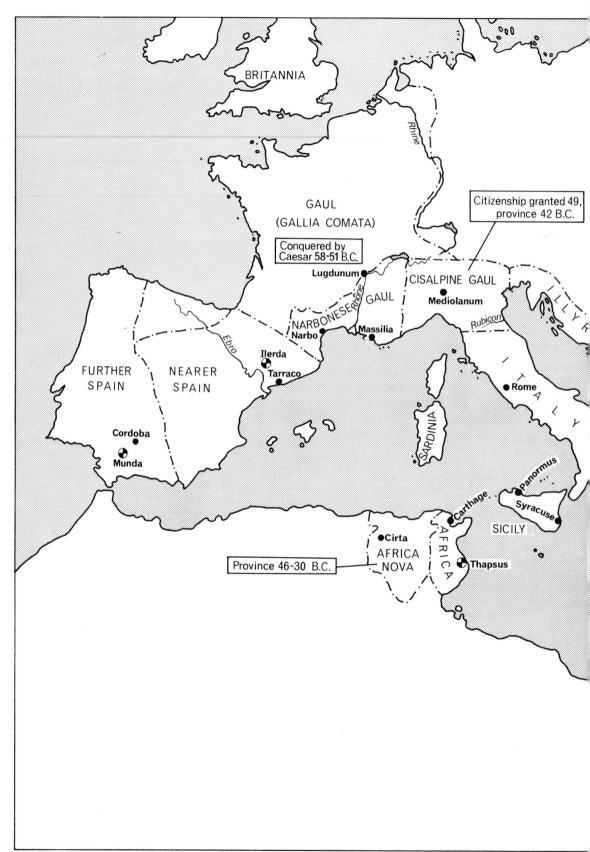

BRITANNIA

Rhine

GAUL
(GALLIA COMATA)

Conquered by
Caesar 58-51 B.C.

Citizenship granted 49,
province 42 B.C.

Lugdunum

CISALPINE GAUL

Mediolanum

Rubicon

NARBONESE GAUL

Rhône

Narbo

Massilia

I L L Y R

Ebro

Ilerda

Tarraco

FURTHER
SPAIN

NEARER
SPAIN

I T A L Y

Rome

SARDINIA

Cordoba

Munda

Panormus

Carthage

Syracuse

SICILY

Cirta

AFRICA
NOVA

A F R I C A

Thapsus

Province 46-30 B.C.

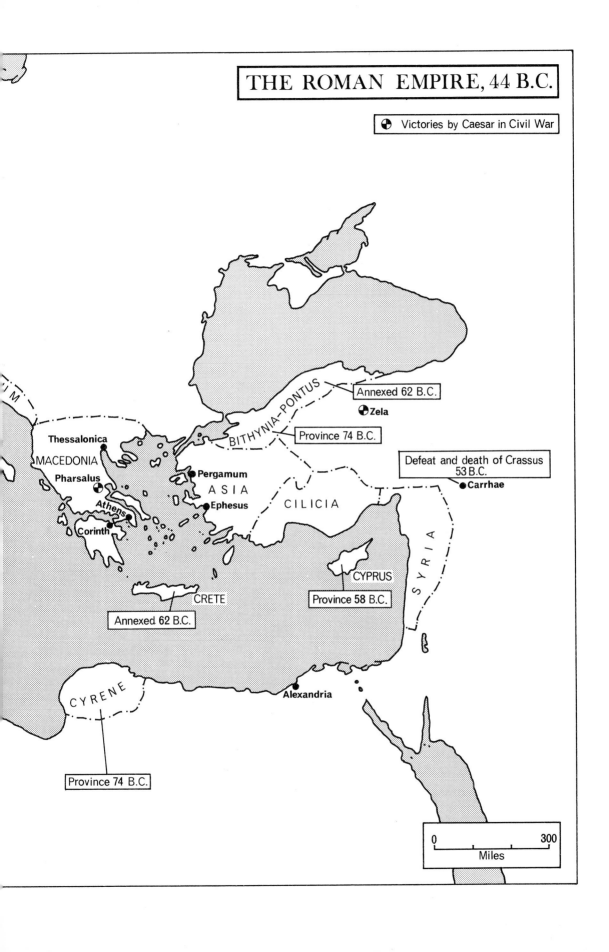

THE ROMAN EMPIRE, 44 B.C.

🌓 Victories by Caesar in Civil War

Annexed 62 B.C.

BITHYNIA-PONTUS

🌓 **Zela**

Province 74 B.C.

Defeat and death of Crassus
53 B.C.

Thessalonica

MACEDONIA

Pharsalus 🌓

Pergamum

A S I A

C I L I C I A

● **Carrhae**

S Y R I A

Athens

Ephesus

Corinth

CYPRUS

CRETE

Province 58 B.C.

Annexed 62 B.C.

C Y R E N E

Alexandria

Province 74 B.C.

0   300
Miles

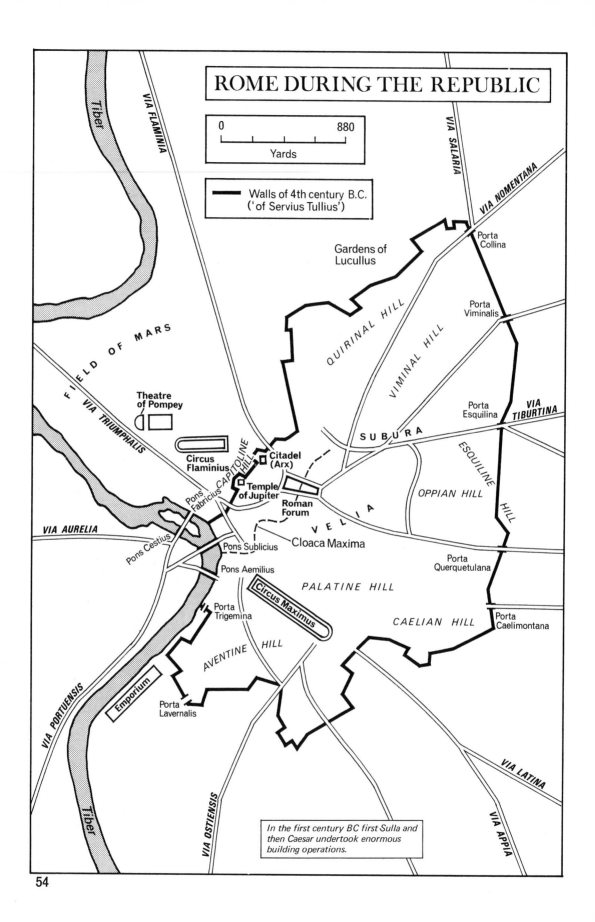

ROME DURING THE REPUBLIC

0 **|** **|** **|** 880
Yards

━━━ Walls of 4th century B.C.
('of Servius Tullius')

Tiber

VIA FLAMINIA

VIA SALARIA

VIA NOMENTANA

Porta
Collina

Gardens of
Lucullus

Porta
Viminalis

F I E L D   O F   M A R S

QUIRINAL HILL

VIMINAL HILL

VIA TRIUMPHALIS

Theatre
of Pompey

Porta
Esquilina

VIA
TIBURTINA

Circus
Flaminius

CAPITOLINE HILL

Citadel
(Arx)

SUBURA

ESQUILINE
HILL

Pons
Fabricius

Temple
of Jupiter

Roman
Forum

OPPIAN HILL

VIA AURELIA

Pons Cestius

V E L I A

Pons Sublicius

Cloaca Maxima

Porta
Querquetulana

Pons Aemilius

PALATINE HILL

Porta
Trigemina

Circus Maximus

CAELIAN HILL

Porta
Caelimontana

Emporium

AVENTINE   HILL

Porta
Lavernalis

VIA PORTUENSIS

VIA OSTIENSIS

VIA LATINA

VIA APPIA

Tiber

*In the first century BC first Sulla and
then Caesar undertook enormous
building operations.*

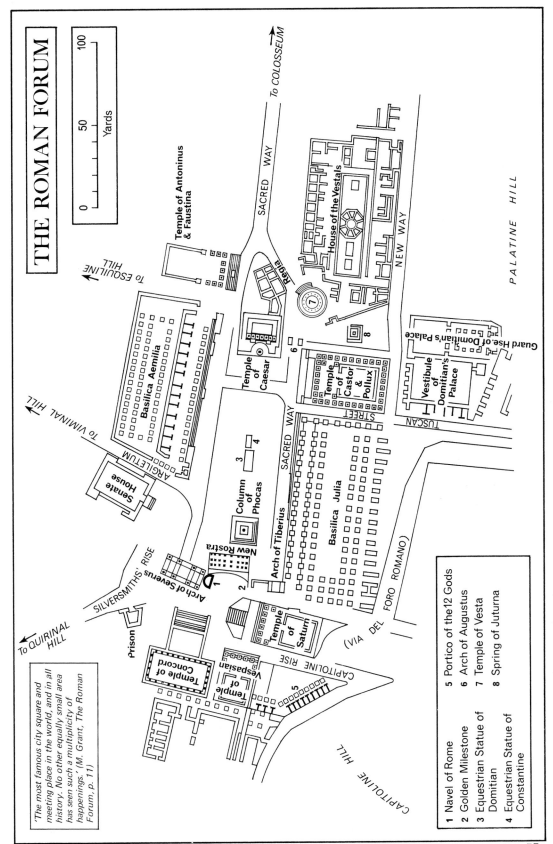

THE ROMAN FORUM

Yards

0   50   100

'The most famous city square and meeting place in the world, and in all history. No other equally small area has seen such a multiplicity of happenings.' (M. Grant, The Roman Forum, p. 11)

To QUIRINAL HILL

To VIMINAL HILL

To ESQUILINE HILL

To COLOSSEUM

Temple of Antoninus & Faustina

Basilica Aemilia

Senate House

ARGILETUM

SILVERSMITHS' RISE

Prison

Temple of Concord

Temple of Vespasian

Temple of Saturn

Arch of Severus

New Rostra

Column of Phocas

Arch of Tiberius

Basilica Julia

Temple of Caesar

Regia

SACRED WAY

Temple of Castor & Pollux

TUSCAN STREET

House of the Vestals

NEW WAY

Guard Hse. of Domitian's Palace

Vestibule of Domitian's Palace

PALATINE HILL

CAPITOLINE RISE

(VIA DEL FORO ROMANO)

CAPITOLINE HILL

3 4

7

8

6

1

2

5

1 Navel of Rome
2 Golden Milestone
3 Equestrian Statue of Domitian
4 Equestrian Statue of Constantine
5 Portico of the 12 Gods
6 Arch of Augustus
7 Temple of Vesta
8 Spring of Juturna

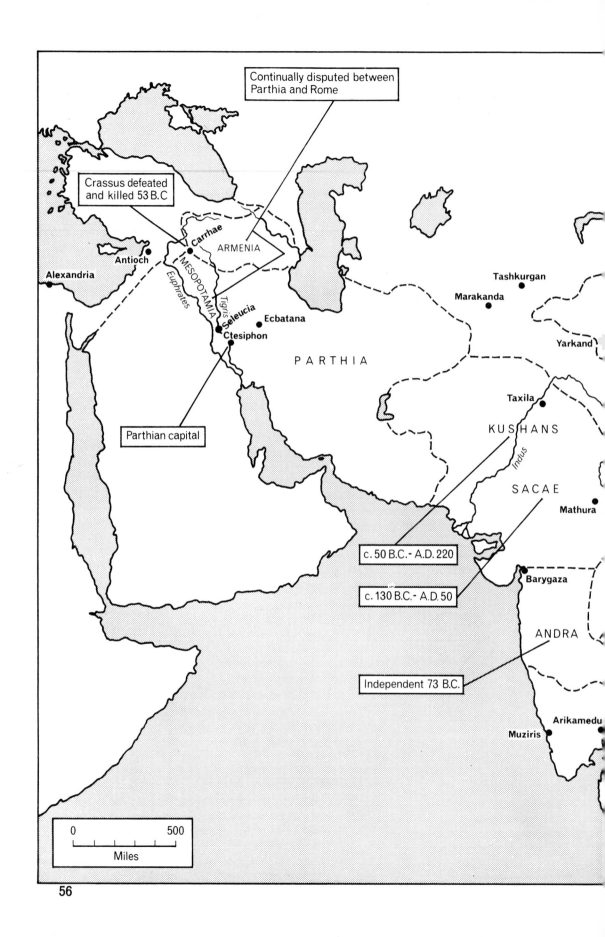

Continually disputed between
Parthia and Rome

Crassus defeated
and killed 53 B.C

Parthian capital

Alexandria

Antioch

Carrhae

ARMENIA

MESOPOTAMIA

Euphrates

Tigris

Seleucia

Ctesiphon

Ecbatana

PARTHIA

Tashkurgan

Marakanda

Yarkand

Taxila

KUSHANS

Indus

SACAE

Mathura

c. 50 B.C.- A.D. 220

c. 130 B.C.- A.D. 50

Barygaza

ANDRA

Independent 73 B.C.

Arikamedu

Muziris

0   500

Miles

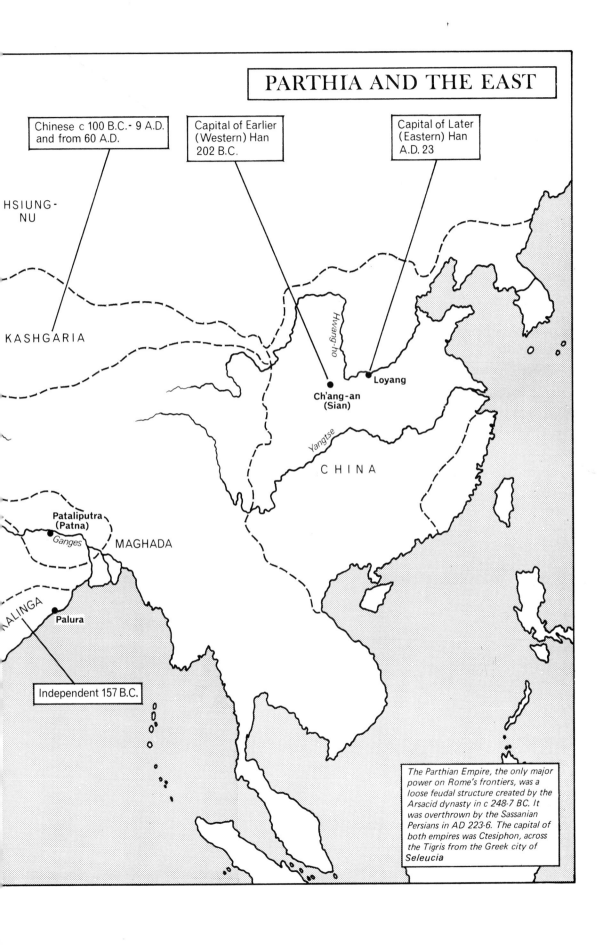

PARTHIA AND THE EAST

Chinese c 100 B.C.- 9 A.D. and from 60 A.D.

Capital of Earlier (Western) Han 202 B.C.

Capital of Later (Eastern) Han A.D. 23

HSIUNG-NU

KASHGARIA

Hwang-ho

Loyang

Ch'ang-an (Sian)

Yangtse

CHINA

Pataliputra (Patna)

Ganges

MAGHADA

KALINGA

Palura

Independent 157 B.C.

The Parthian Empire, the only major power on Rome's frontiers, was a loose feudal structure created by the Arsacid dynasty in c 248-7 BC. It was overthrown by the Sassanian Persians in AD 223-6. The capital of both empires was Ctesiphon, across the Tigris from the Greek city of **Seleucia**

BRITANNIA

LWR.
GERMANY
(17 B.C.)

FREE
GERMANY

Temporarily conquered from
15 B.C. but abandoned after
ambushing of Varus by
Arminius in A.D. 9

Colonia
Agrippinensis

Rhine

B E L G I C A

Moguntiacum

Danube

LOWER
PANNONIA
(10
B.C.)

LUGDUNENSIS

RHAETIA
(15 B.C.)

NORICUM
(15 B.C.)

UPPER
PANNONIA

UPR.
GERMANY
(17 B.C.)

Lugdunum

P

Aquileia

I
T
A
L
Y

AQUITANIA

C

M

NARBONENSIS

Nemausus

Adriatic
Sea

Rome

T A R R A C O N E N S I S

Tarraco

LUSITANIA
(c. 27 B.C.)

Corduba

BAETICA

Gades

Naulochus

SICILY

Carthage

M A U R E T A N I A

Naval victory over
Sextus Pompeius
36 B.C.

A
F
R
I
C
A

Imperial frontier as in A.D. 14

- - - - Provincial frontiers

ASIA   Senatorial provinces

ALPINE PROVINCES (15-14 B.C.)
M: Maritime, C: Cottian, P: Pennine

*The hatched areas represent the
more important dependent ('client')
states, whose monarchs enjoyed
internal autonomy but had to
support Rome's foreign policy and
help defend the imperial frontiers.*

Principal client states

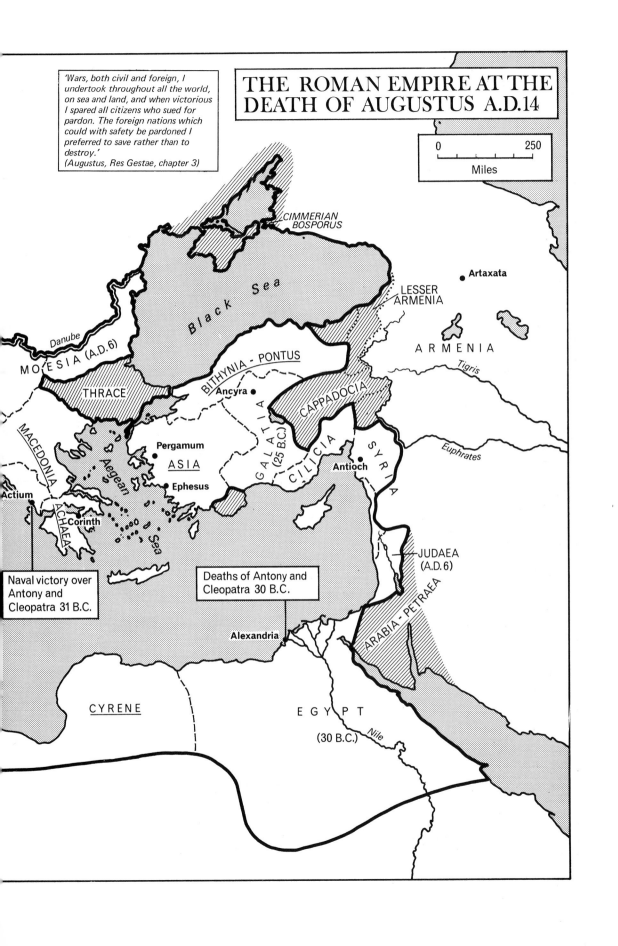

THE ROMAN EMPIRE AT THE DEATH OF AUGUSTUS A.D.14

'Wars, both civil and foreign, I undertook throughout all the world, on sea and land, and when victorious I spared all citizens who sued for pardon. The foreign nations which could with safety be pardoned I preferred to save rather than to destroy.'
(Augustus, Res Gestae, chapter 3)

0   250
Miles

CIMMERIAN BOSPORUS

Black Sea

• Artaxata

LESSER ARMENIA

Danube

MOESIA (A.D.6)

A R M E N I A

Tigris

THRACE

BITHYNIA - PONTUS

Ancyra •

CAPPADOCIA

MACEDONIA

Pergamum

ASIA

GALATIA (25 B.C.)

CILICIA

SYRIA

Antioch •

Euphrates

Aegean Sea

Ephesus •

Actium

ACHAEA

Corinth •

Cyprus

JUDAEA (A.D.6)

Naval victory over Antony and Cleopatra 31 B.C.

Deaths of Antony and Cleopatra 30 B.C.

ARABIA - PETRAEA

Alexandria

CYRENE

E G Y P T

(30 B.C.)

Nile

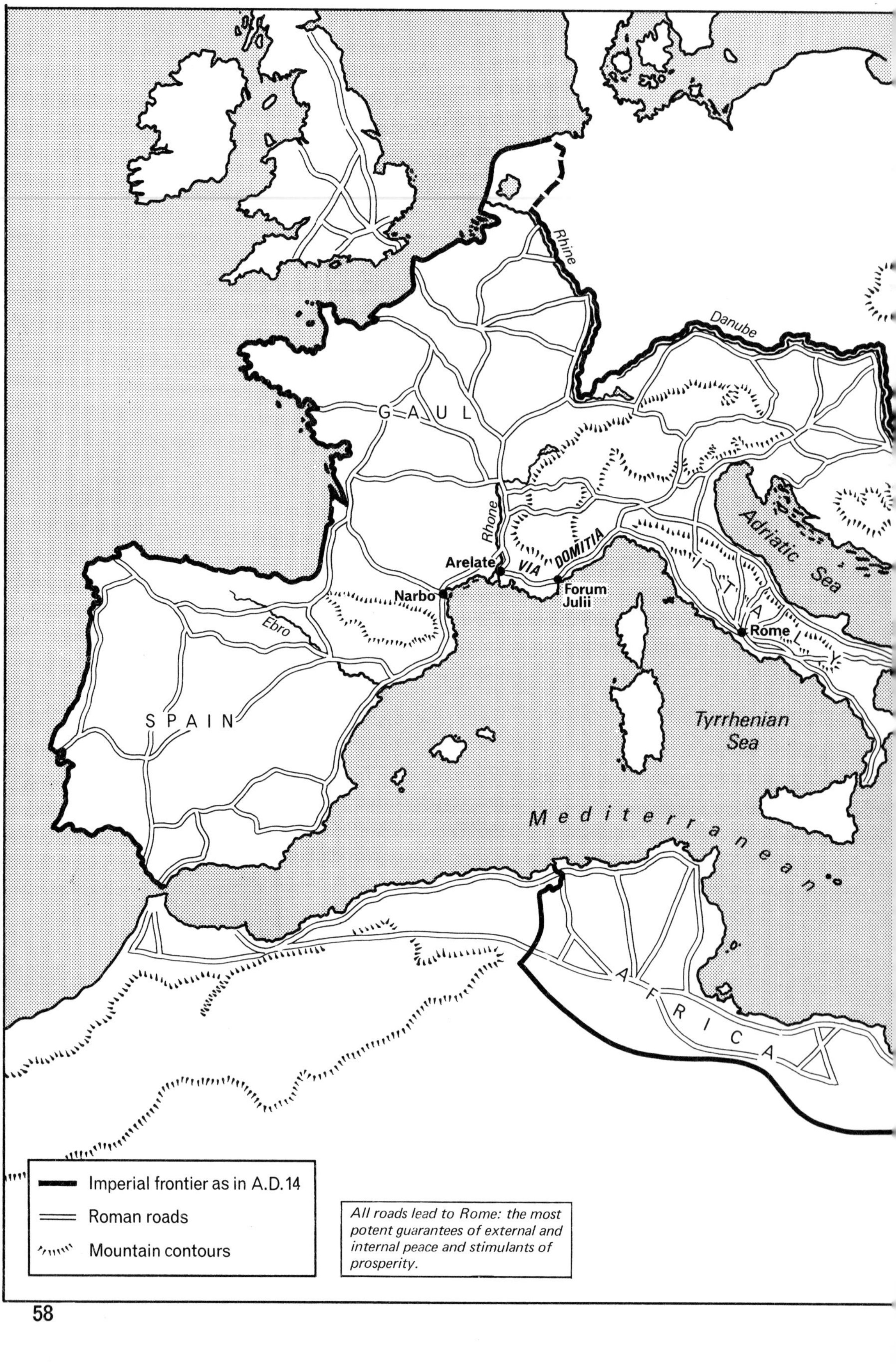

Rhine
Danube
GAUL
Rhone
Arelate
VIA DOMITIA
Forum Julii
Narbo
Ebro
SPAIN
ITALY
Adriatic Sea
Rome
Tyrrhenian Sea
Mediterranean
AFRICA
Imperial frontier as in A.D.14
Roman roads
Mountain contours

All roads lead to Rome: the most potent guarantees of external and internal peace and stimulants of prosperity.

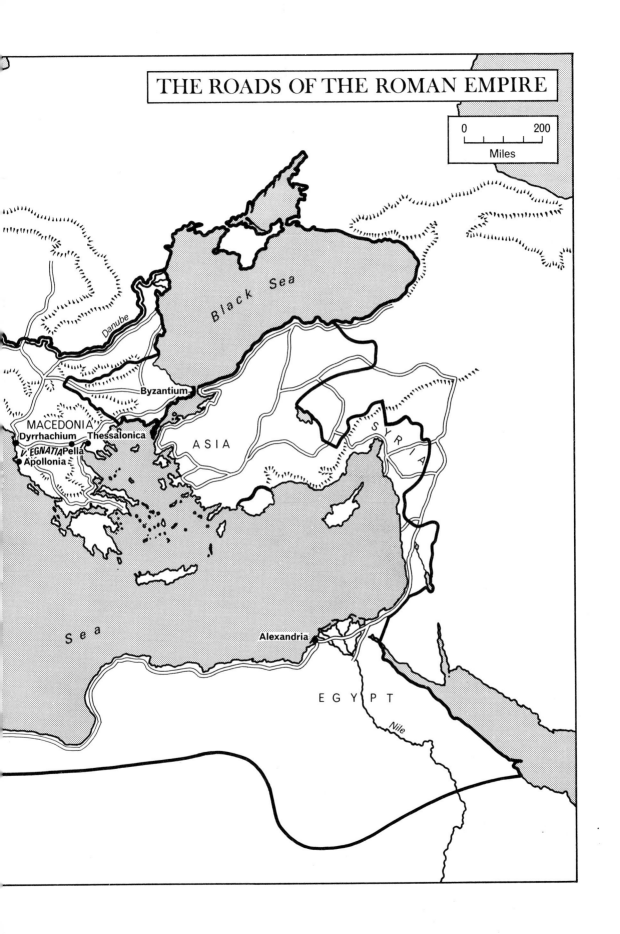

THE ROADS OF THE ROMAN EMPIRE

0 — 200
Miles

Black Sea

Danube

Byzantium

MACEDONIA

Dyrrhachium

*V. EGNATIA***Pella**

Apollonia

Thessalonica

ASIA

S Y R I A

Sea

Alexandria

E G Y P T

Nile

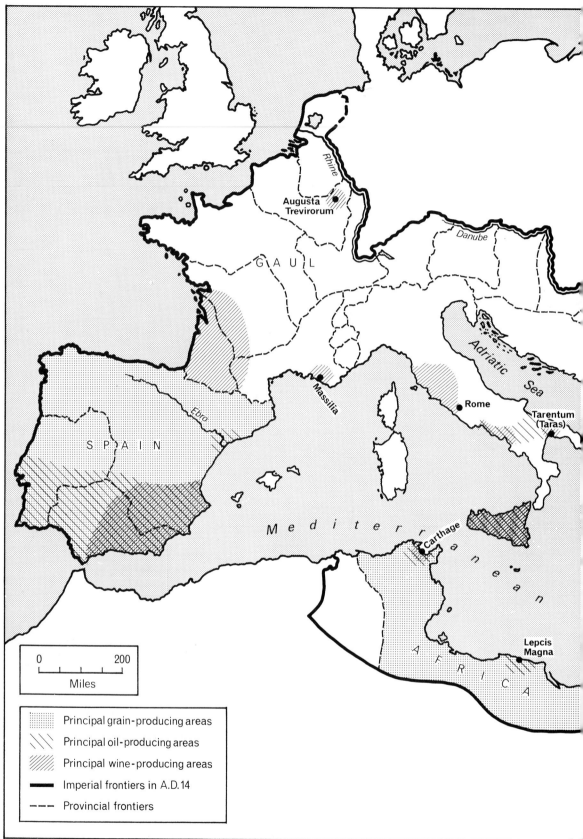

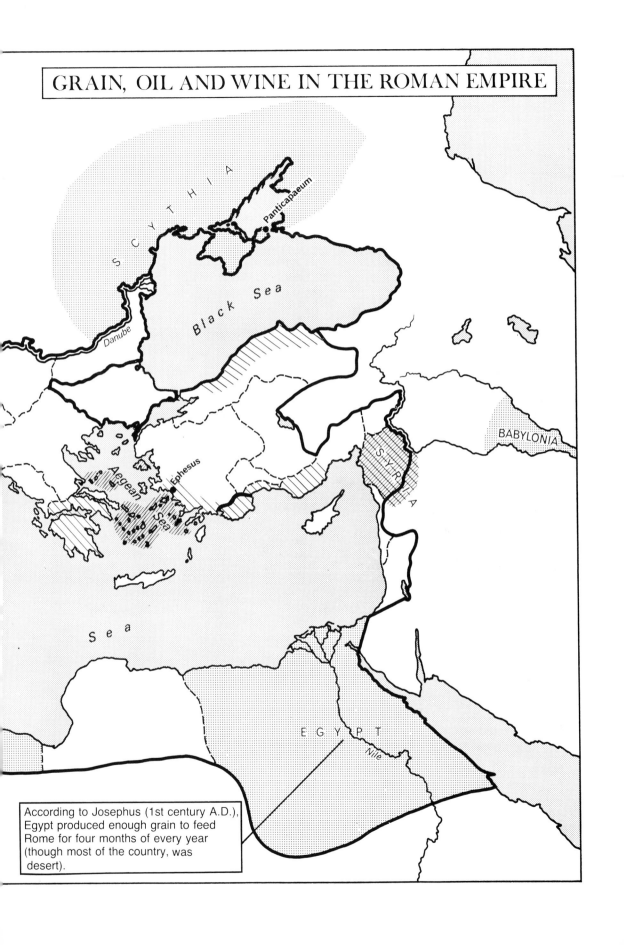

GRAIN, OIL AND WINE IN THE ROMAN EMPIRE

S C Y T H I A

Panticapaeum

Danube

Black Sea

BABYLONIA

S
Y
R
I
A

Aegean
Sea

Ephesus

Sea

E G Y P T

Nile

According to Josephus (1st century A.D.),
Egypt produced enough grain to feed
Rome for four months of every year
(though most of the country, was
desert).

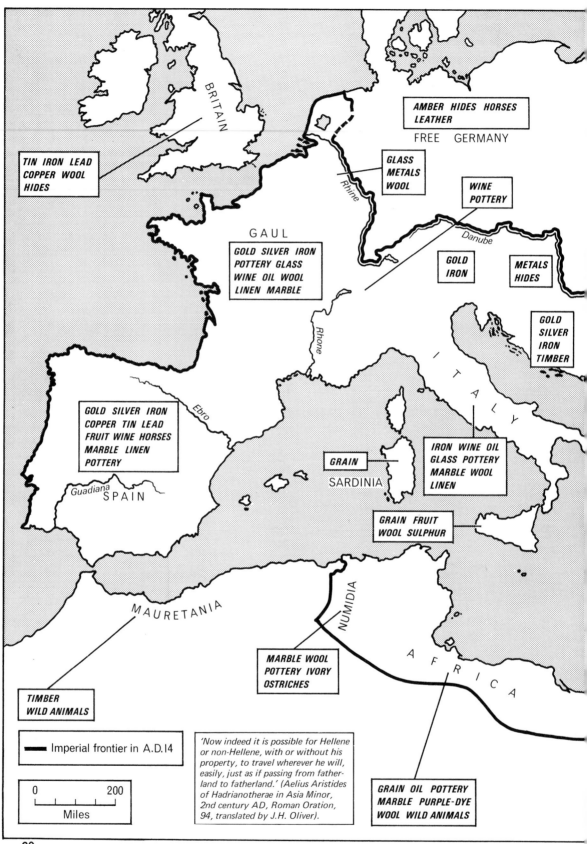

BRITAIN

TIN IRON LEAD
COPPER WOOL
HIDES

FREE GERMANY

AMBER HIDES HORSES
LEATHER

GLASS
METALS
WOOL

WINE
POTTERY

GAUL

GOLD SILVER IRON
POTTERY GLASS
WINE OIL WOOL
LINEN MARBLE

Rhine

Danube

GOLD
IRON

METALS
HIDES

Rhone

GOLD
SILVER
IRON
TIMBER

I T A L Y

Ebro

GOLD SILVER IRON
COPPER TIN LEAD
FRUIT WINE HORSES
MARBLE LINEN
POTTERY

Guadiana SPAIN

GRAIN

SARDINIA

IRON WINE OIL
GLASS POTTERY
MARBLE WOOL
LINEN

GRAIN FRUIT
WOOL SULPHUR

MAURETANIA

NUMIDIA

A F R I C A

MARBLE WOOL
POTTERY IVORY
OSTRICHES

TIMBER
WILD ANIMALS

Imperial frontier in A.D.14

'Now indeed it is possible for Hellene
or non-Hellene, with or without his
property, to travel wherever he will,
easily, just as if passing from fatherland to fatherland.' (Aelius Aristides
of Hadrianotherae in Asia Minor,
2nd century AD, Roman Oration,
94, translated by J.H. Oliver).

0   200
Miles

GRAIN OIL POTTERY
MARBLE PURPLE-DYE
WOOL WILD ANIMALS

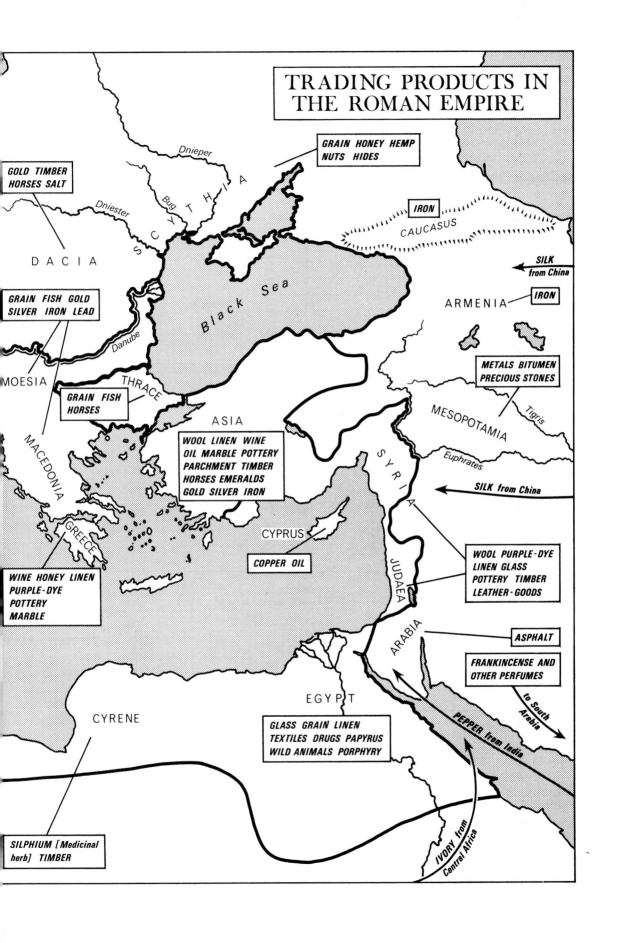

TRADING PRODUCTS IN THE ROMAN EMPIRE

GOLD TIMBER
HORSES SALT

GRAIN HONEY HEMP
NUTS HIDES

Dnieper

Dniester

Bug

S C Y T H I A

IRON

CAUCASUS

SILK
from China

D A C I A

ARMENIA

IRON

GRAIN FISH GOLD
SILVER IRON LEAD

Danube

Black Sea

METALS BITUMEN
PRECIOUS STONES

MESOPOTAMIA

Tigris

MOESIA

THRACE

GRAIN FISH
HORSES

ASIA

WOOL LINEN WINE
OIL MARBLE POTTERY
PARCHMENT TIMBER
HORSES EMERALDS
GOLD SILVER IRON

S
Y
R
I
A

Euphrates

SILK from China

MACEDONIA

GREECE

CYPRUS

COPPER OIL

J
U
D
A
E
A

WOOL PURPLE-DYE
LINEN GLASS
POTTERY TIMBER
LEATHER-GOODS

WINE HONEY LINEN
PURPLE-DYE
POTTERY
MARBLE

A
R
A
B
I
A

ASPHALT

FRANKINCENSE AND
OTHER PERFUMES

to South
Arabia

CYRENE

EGYPT

GLASS GRAIN LINEN
TEXTILES DRUGS PAPYRUS
WILD ANIMALS PORPHYRY

PEPPER from India

SILPHIUM [Medicinal
herb] TIMBER

*IVORY from
Central Africa*

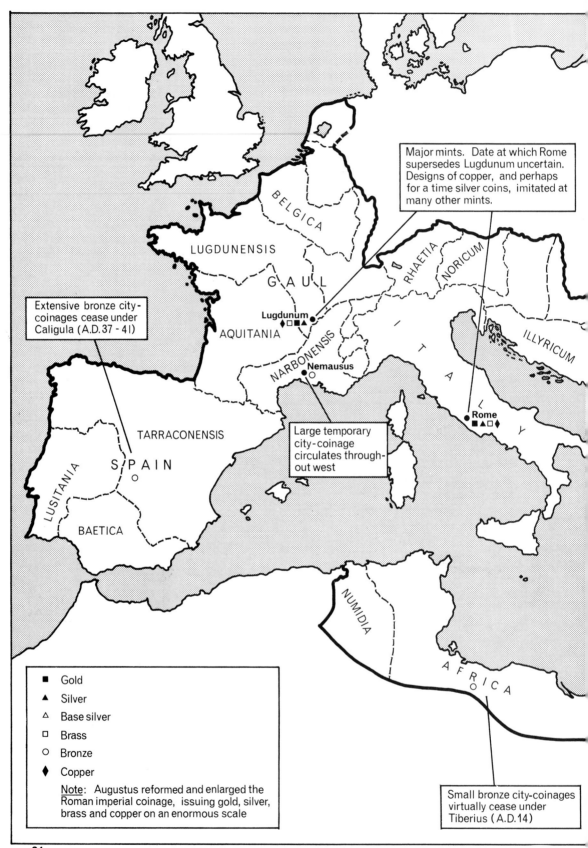

Major mints. Date at which Rome
supersedes Lugdunum uncertain.
Designs of copper, and perhaps
for a time silver coins, imitated at
many other mints.

Extensive bronze city-
coinages cease under
Caligula (A.D. 37 - 41)

Large temporary
city-coinage
circulates through-
out west

■ Gold

▲ Silver

△ Base silver

□ Brass

○ Bronze

◆ Copper

Note: Augustus reformed and enlarged the
Roman imperial coinage, issuing gold, silver,
brass and copper on an enormous scale

Small bronze city-coinages
virtually cease under
Tiberius (A.D. 14)

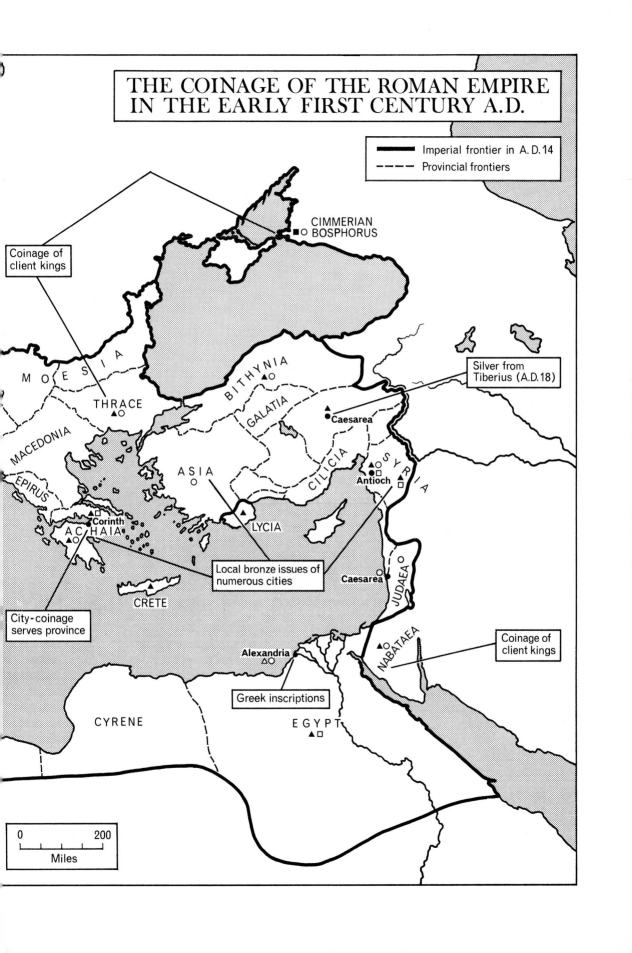

THE COINAGE OF THE ROMAN EMPIRE
IN THE EARLY FIRST CENTURY A.D.

—— Imperial frontier in A.D.14
- - - Provincial frontiers

CIMMERIAN
BOSPHORUS

Coinage of
client kings

Silver from
Tiberius (A.D.18)

M O E S I A

THRACE

BITHYNIA

GALATIA

Caesarea

MACEDONIA

CILICIA

SYRIA

EPIRUS

ASIA

Antioch

Corinth

ACHAIA

LYCIA

Local bronze issues of
numerous cities

Caesarea

JUDAEA

City-coinage
serves province

CRETE

Coinage of
client kings

NABATAEA

Alexandria

Greek inscriptions

CYRENE

E G Y P T

0   200
Miles

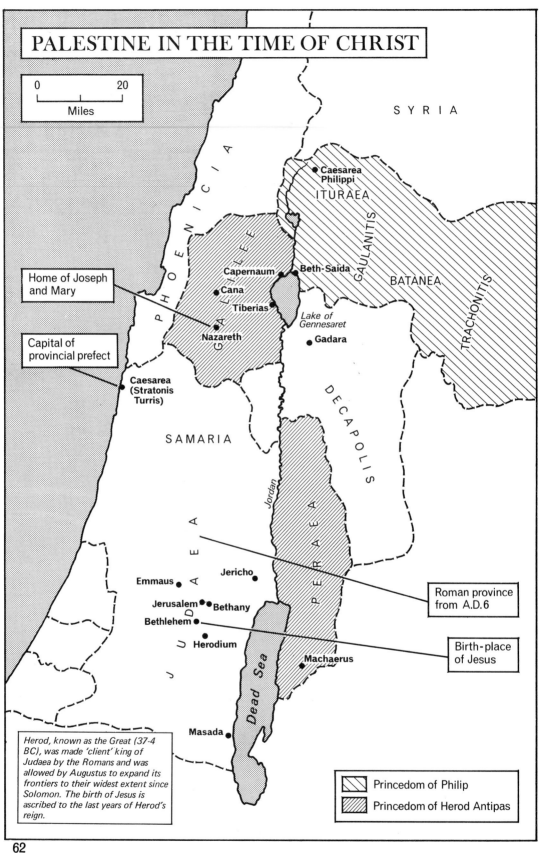

PALESTINE IN THE TIME OF CHRIST

0   20
Miles

SYRIA

● Caesarea Philippi

ITURAEA

GAULANITIS

BATANEA

TRACHONITIS

P H O E N I C I A

G A L I L E E

Home of Joseph and Mary

● Capernaum   Beth-Saida ●
● Cana
Tiberias ●

Lake of Gennesaret

Nazareth ●

● Gadara

Capital of provincial prefect

Caesarea (Stratonis Turris) ●

DECAPOLIS

SAMARIA

Jordan

P E R A E A

Roman province from A.D.6

Emmaus ●   J U D A E A   ● Jericho

Jerusalem ●● Bethany
Bethlehem ●

Birth-place of Jesus

Herodium ●

● Machaerus

Dead Sea

Masada ●

Herod, known as the Great (37-4 BC), was made 'client' king of Judaea by the Romans and was allowed by Augustus to expand its frontiers to their widest extent since Solomon. The birth of Jesus is ascribed to the last years of Herod's reign.

▨ Princedom of Philip
▨ Princedom of Herod Antipas

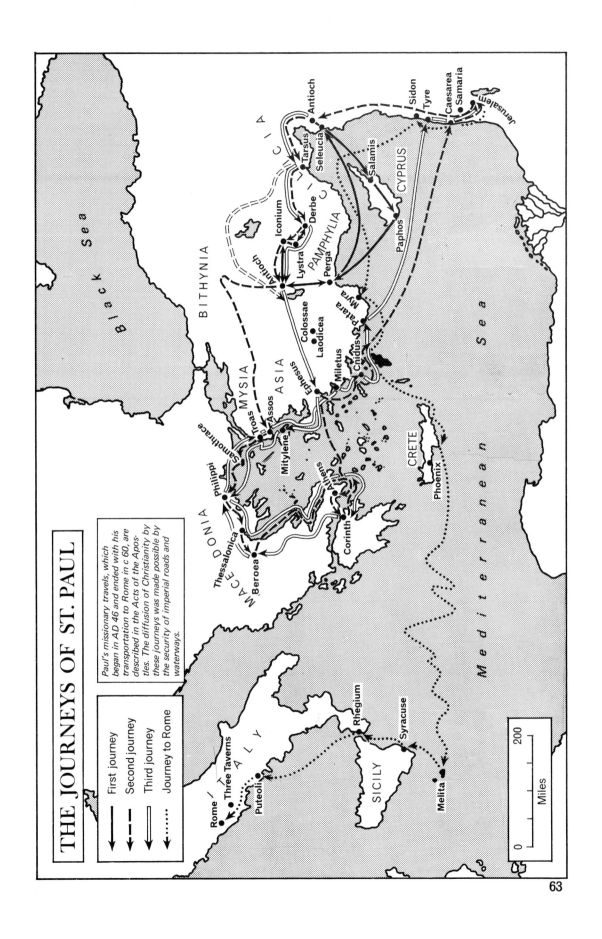

THE JOURNEYS OF ST. PAUL

First journey
Second journey
Third journey
Journey to Rome

*Paul's missionary travels, which
began in AD 46 and ended with his
transportation to Rome in c 60, are
described in the Acts of the Apos-
tles. The diffusion of Christianity by
these journeys was made possible by
the security of imperial roads and
waterways.*

Black Sea

BITHYNIA

MYSIA
ASIA

Troas
Assos
Mitylene

MACEDONIA
Philippi
Thessalonica
Beroea
Samothrace
Athens
Corinth

CRETE
Phoenix

Ephesus
Miletus
Cnidus

Colossae
Laodicea
Patara
Myra

Antioch
Iconium
Derbe
Lystra
PAMPHYLIA
Perga

CILICIA
Tarsus
Seleucia

CYPRUS
Salamis
Paphos

Antioch
Sidon
Tyre
Caesarea
Samaria
Jerusalem

Mediterranean Sea

ITALY
Rome
Three Taverns
Puteoli
Rhegium
Syracuse
SICILY
Melita

Miles
200
0

63

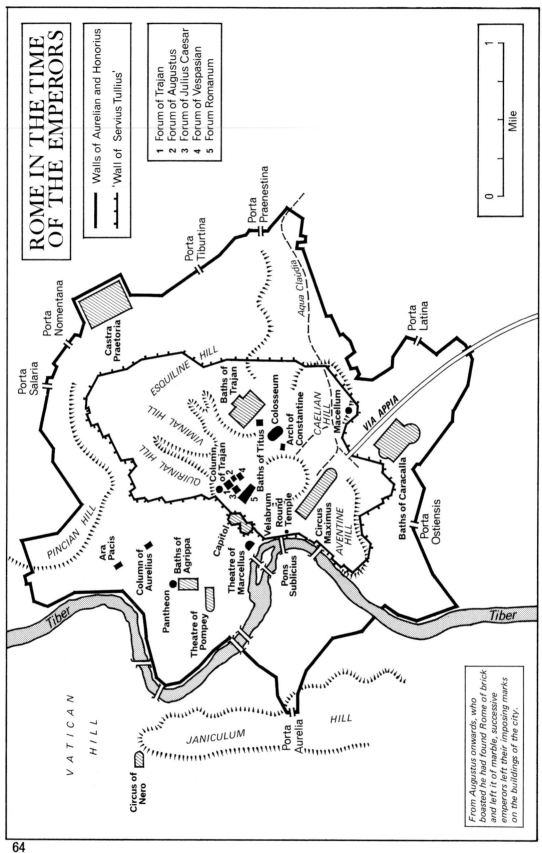

ROME IN THE TIME OF THE EMPERORS

Walls of Aurelian and Honorius

'Wall of Servius Tullius'

1 Forum of Trajan
2 Forum of Augustus
3 Forum of Julius Caesar
4 Forum of Vespasian
5 Forum Romanum

0   1
Mile

Porta Tiburtina

Porta Praenestina

Porta Nomentana

Castra Praetoria

Porta Salaria

ESQUILINE HILL

Baths of Trajan

Aqua Claudia

Porta Latina

VIMINAL HILL

Colosseum

Arch of Constantine

Macellum

CAELIAN HILL

VIA APPIA

QUIRINAL HILL

Column of Trajan

Baths of Titus

PINCIAN HILL

3 2
4
5

Velabrum
Round Temple

Circus Maximus

AVENTINE HILL

Baths of Caracalla

Porta Ostiensis

Ara Pacis

Column of Aurelius

Pantheon

Baths of Agrippa

Theatre of Pompey

Capitol
Theatre of Marcellus

Pons Sublicius

Porta Aurelia

Tiber

VATICAN HILL

JANICULUM HILL

Tiber

Circus of Nero

From Augustus onwards, who boasted he had found Rome of brick and left it of marble, successive emperors left their imposing marks on the buildings of the city.

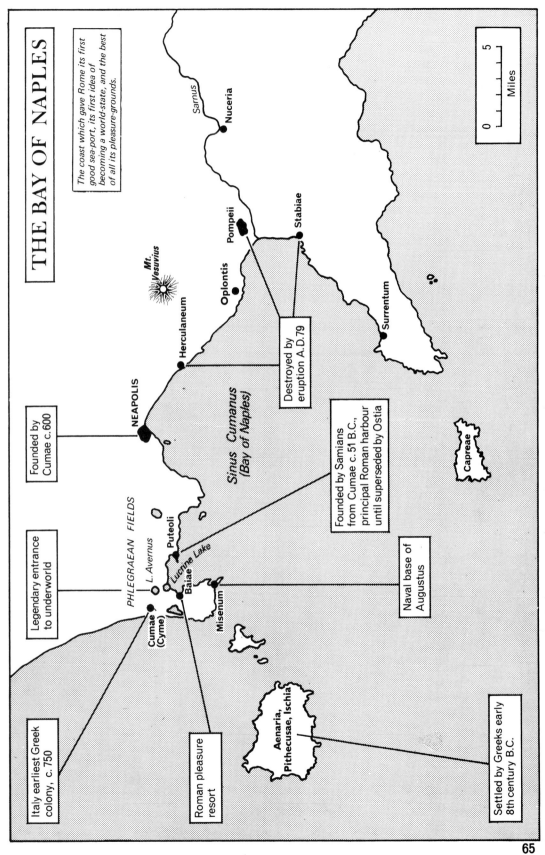

THE BAY OF NAPLES

The coast which gave Rome its first good sea-port, its first idea of becoming a world-state, and the best of all its pleasure-grounds.

Sarnus

Nuceria

Mt. Vesuvius

Pompeii

Oplontis

Stabiae

Herculaneum

Destroyed by eruption A.D.79

Surrentum

NEAPOLIS

Founded by Cumae c. 600

Sinus Cumanus
(Bay of Naples)

Founded by Samians from Cumae c. 51 B.C., principal Roman harbour until superseded by Ostia

Capreae

PHLEGRAEAN FIELDS

Puteoli

L. Avernus

Lucrine Lake

Baiae

Legendary entrance to underworld

Naval base of Augustus

Cumae (Cyme)

Misenum

Italy earliest Greek colony, c. 750

Roman pleasure resort

Aenaria, Pithecusae, Ischia

Settled by Greeks early 8th century B.C.

0   5
Miles

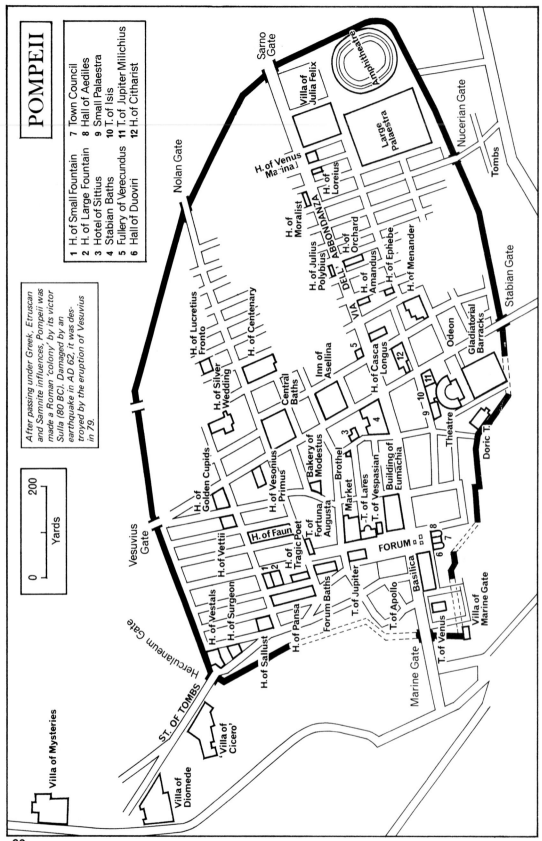

POMPEII

1 H. of Small Fountain
2 H. of Large Fountain
3 Hotel of Sittius
4 Stabian Baths
5 Fullery of Verecundus
6 Hall of Duoviri
7 Town Council
8 Hall of Aediles
9 Small Palaestra
10 T. of Isis
11 T. of Jupiter Milichius
12 H. of Citharist

After passing under Greek, Etruscan and Samnite influences, Pompeii was made a Roman 'colony' by its victor Sulla (80 BC). Damaged by an earthquake in AD 62, it was destroyed by the eruption of Vesuvius in 79.

0   200
Yards

Sarno Gate

Amphitheatre

Villa of Julia Felix

Nucerian Gate

Large Palaestra

Tombs

Nolan Gate

H. of Venus Marina

H. of Loreius

Stabian Gate

H. of Moralist

DELL' ABBONDANZA

H. of Orchard

H. of Julius Polybius

VIA

H. of Amandus

H. of Ephebe

H. of Menander

H. of Lucretius Fronto

H. of Centenary

5

H. of Casca Longus

12

Odeon

Gladiatorial Barracks

H. of Silver Wedding

Central Baths

Inn of Asellina

11

9–10

Theatre

Doric T.

H. of Golden Cupids

H. of Vesonius Primus

Bakery of Modestus

3

4

H. of Faun

T. of Fortuna Augusta

Brothel

Market

T. of Lares

T. of Vespasian

Building of Eumachia

8
7
6

Vesuvius Gate

H. of Vettii

H. of Tragic Poet

FORUM

H. of Vestals

H. of Surgeon

H. of Pansa

Forum Baths

T. of Jupiter

Basilica

T. of Apollo

Villa of Marine Gate

1
2

H. of Sallust

Marine Gate

T. of Venus

Herculaneum Gate

ST. OF TOMBS

'Villa of Cicero'

Villa of Diomede

Villa of Mysteries

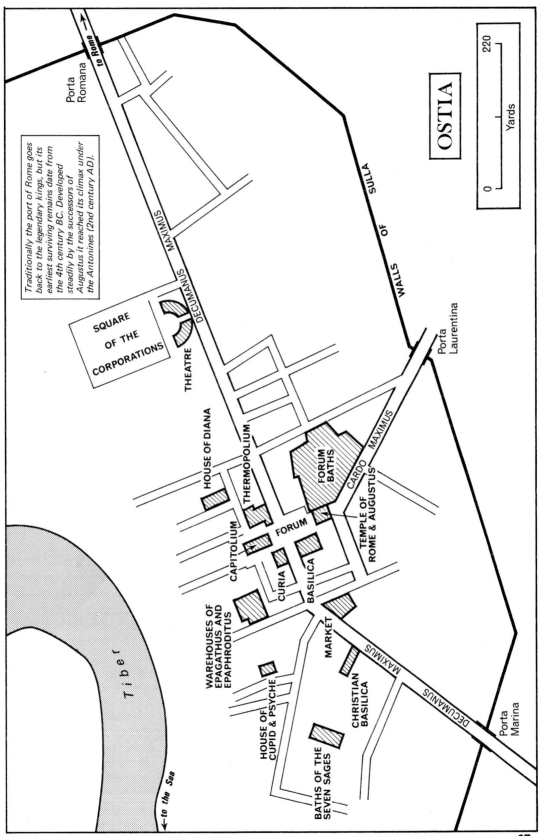

OSTIA

Yards

0 ——— 220

Porta Romana

to Rome →

Traditionally the port of Rome goes back to the legendary kings, but its earliest surviving remains date from the 4th century BC. Developed steadily by the successors of Augustus it reached its climax under the Antonines (2nd century AD).

SQUARE OF THE CORPORATIONS

THEATRE

DECUMANUS MAXIMUS

WALLS OF SULLA

Porta Laurentina

HOUSE OF DIANA

THERMOPOLIUM

CAPITOLIUM

FORUM BATHS

FORUM

CURIA

BASILICA

TEMPLE OF ROME & AUGUSTUS

CARDO MAXIMUS

WAREHOUSES OF EPAGATHUS AND EPAPHRODITUS

MARKET

HOUSE OF CUPID & PSYCHE

CHRISTIAN BASILICA

DECUMANUS MAXIMUS

Porta Marina

BATHS OF THE SEVEN SAGES

Tiber

← to the Sea

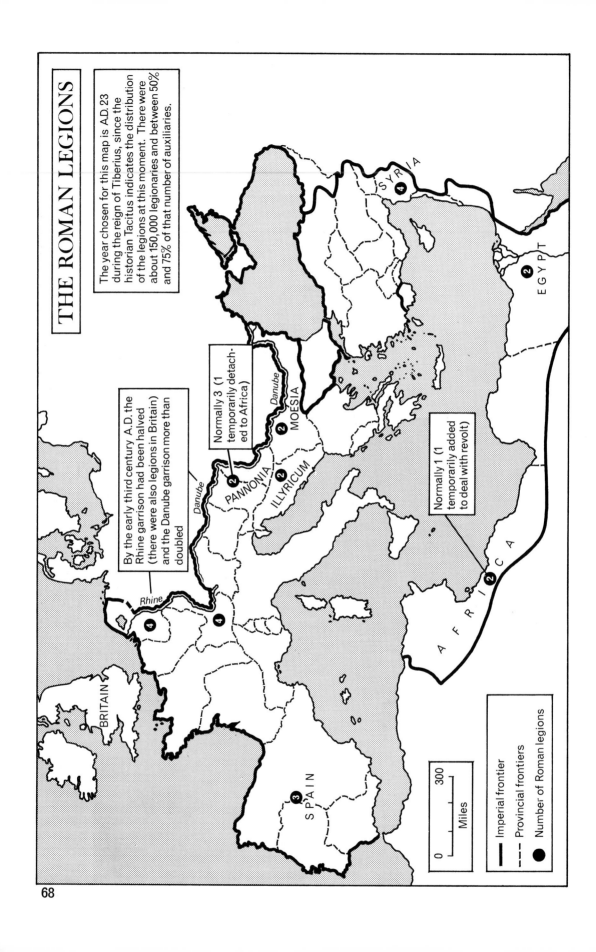

THE ROMAN LEGIONS

The year chosen for this map is A.D. 23 during the reign of Tiberius, since the historian Tacitus indicates the distribution of the legions at this moment. There were about 150,000 legionaries and between 50% and 75% of that number of auxiliaries.

Normally 3 (1 temporarily detach-ed to Africa)

By the early third century A.D. the Rhine garrison had been halved (there were also legions in Britain) and the Danube garrison more than doubled

Normally 1 (1 temporarily added to deal with revolt)

Danube

Danube

Rhine

MOESIA

PANNONIA

ILLYRICUM

BRITAIN

SPAIN

A F R I C A

E G Y P T

S Y R I A

— Imperial frontier
--- Provincial frontiers
● Number of Roman legions

0   300
Miles

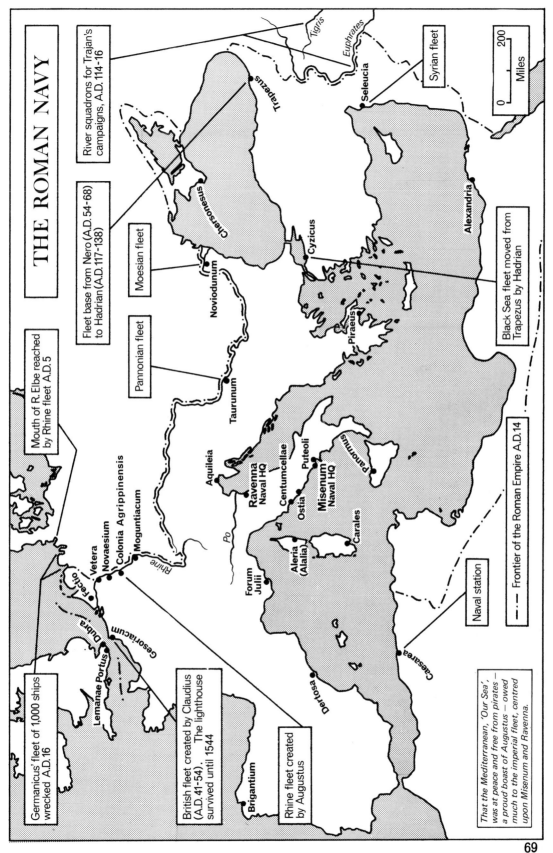

THE ROMAN NAVY

River squadrons for Trajan's campaigns, A.D. 114-16

Syrian fleet

Fleet base from Nero (A.D. 54-68) to Hadrian (A.D. 117-138)

Moesian fleet

Pannonian fleet

Black Sea fleet moved from Trapezus by Hadrian

Mouth of R. Elbe reached by Rhine fleet A.D. 5

Germanicus' fleet of 1,000 ships wrecked A.D. 16

British fleet created by Claudius (A.D. 41-54). The lighthouse survived until 1544

Rhine fleet created by Augustus

Naval station

– · – Frontier of the Roman Empire A.D. 14

Naval station

That the Mediterranean, 'Our Sea', was at peace and free from pirates — a proud boast of Augustus — owed much to the imperial fleet, centred upon Misenum and Ravenna.

Tigris

Euphrates

Seleucia

200

0   Miles

Trapezus

Alexandria

Chersonesus

Cyzicus

Noviodunum

Piraeus

Taurunum

Aquileia

Ravenna Naval HQ

Centumcellae

Puteoli

Ostia

Misenum Naval HQ

Carrales

Aleria (Alalia)

Pandateria

Forum Julii

Detosa

Caesarea

Po

Rhine

Vetera

Novaesium

Colonia Agrippinensis

Moguntiacum

Fectio

Dubra

Gesoriacum

Lemanae Portus

Brigantium

69

BRITANNIA (AD 71)
(AD 59)
(AD 43-47)
Londinium

FREE GERMANY

LOWER GERMANY
Colonia Agrippinensis

Moguntiacum

Rhine

AGRI DECUMAT. (83)

LUGDUNENSIS

UPPER GERMANY

RHAETIA

NORICUM

Danube

PANNONIA UPPER

LOWER

GALLIA

Lugdunum

AQUITANIA

NARBONENSIS

Aquileia

Adriatic Sea

ILLYRICUM

Nemausus

I T A L I A

TARRACONENSIS

Tarraco

Rome

HISPANIA

LUSITANIA

SARDINIA

BAETICA

Corduba

Gades

SICILY

Carthage

MAURETANIA (A.D. 42)

A F R I C A

Frontier of Roman Empire A.D. 14
Frontier of Roman Empire A.D. 117
Province boundaries

THE ROMAN EMPIRE FROM TIBERIUS (A.D.14-37) TO TRAJAN (98-117)

Trajan's expansion as far as the Persian Gulf came to nothing, since his successor Hadrian withdrew to the Euphrates again.

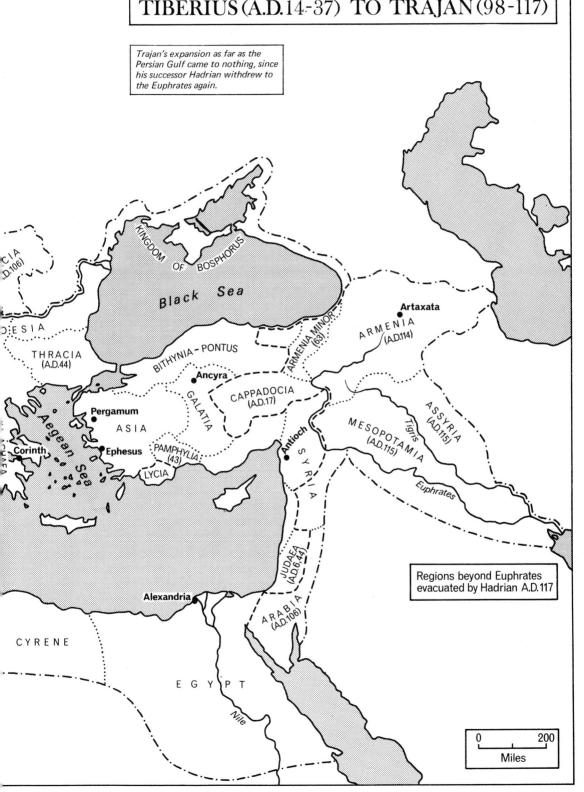

KINGDOM OF BOSPHORUS

Black Sea

Artaxata

ARMENIA (A.D.114)

ARMENIA MINOR (63)

THRACIA (A.D.44)

BITHYNIA - PONTUS

Ancyra

ASSYRIA (A.D.115)

CAPPADOCIA (A.D.17)

GALATIA

Tigris

MESOPOTAMIA (A.D.115)

Pergamum

ASIA

Aegean Sea

Antioch

Corinth

Ephesus

PAMPHYLIA (43)

LYCIA

SYRIA

Euphrates

JUDAEA (A.D.6,44)

Alexandria

ARABIA (A.D.106)

Regions beyond Euphrates evacuated by Hadrian A.D.117

CYRENE

E G Y P T

Nile

0   200
Miles

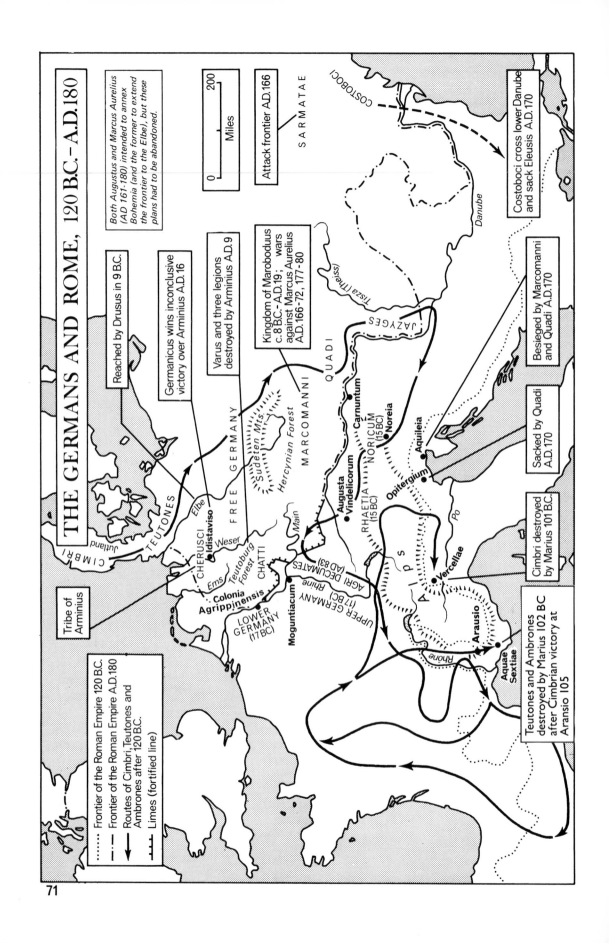

THE GERMANS AND ROME, 120 B.C.–A.D.180

Both Augustus and Marcus Aurelius (AD 161-180) intended to extend the frontier to the Elbe), but these plans had to be abandoned.

0 _____ 200
Miles

Attack frontier A.D.166

Reached by Drusus in 9 B.C.

Germanicus wins inconclusive victory over Arminius A.D.16

Varus and three legions destroyed by Arminius A.D.9

Kingdom of Maroboduus c.8 BC.-AD.19; wars against Marcus Aurelius A.D.166-72, 177-80

Costoboci cross lower Danube and sack Eleusis A.D.170

Besieged by Marcomanni and Quadi A.D.170

Sacked by Quadi A.D.170

Cimbri destroyed by Marius 101 B.C.

Teutones and Ambrones destroyed by Marius 102 BC after Cimbrian victory at Aransio 105

Tribe of Arminius

.... Frontier of the Roman Empire 120 B.C.
–·–·– Frontier of the Roman Empire A.D.180
↓ Routes of Cimbri,Teutones and Ambrones after 120 B.C.
┴┴┴ Limes (fortified line)

COSTOBOCI

SARMATAE

Danube

JAZYGES

Tisza (Theiss)

QUADI

MARCOMANNI

FREE GERMANY

Sudeten Mts.

Hercynian Forest

TEUTONES

CIMBRI

Jutland

CHERUSCI

Elbe

Idistaviso

Weser

Ems

Teutoburg Forest

CHATTI

Colonia Agrippinensis

LOWER GERMANY (17BC)

Moguntiacum

Main

Rhine

AGRI DECUMATES (AD 83)

UPPER GERMANY (17BC)

RHAETIA (15BC)

Augusta Vindelicorum

NORICUM (15BC)

Carnuntum

Noreia

Aquileia

Opitergium

A L P S

Po

Vercellae

Rhone

Arausio

Aquae Sextiae

71

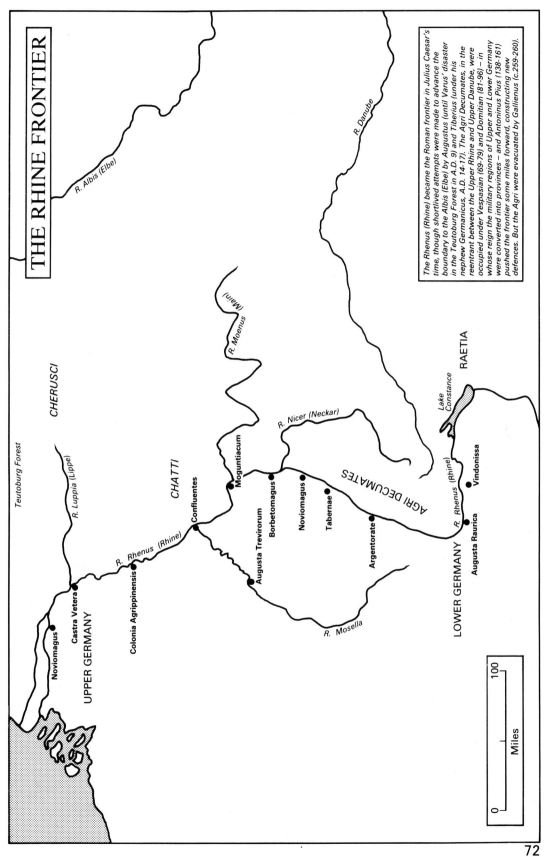

THE RHINE FRONTIER

Teutoburg Forest

CHERUSCI

R. Albis (Elbe)

R. Danube

R. Luppia (Lippe)

R. Rhenus (Rhine)

Noviomagus

Castra Vetera

UPPER GERMANY

Colonia Agrippinensis

CHATTI

Confluentes

Augusta Trevirorum

R. Mosella

Moguntiacum

Borbetomagus

Noviomagus

Tabernae

Argentorate

R. Moenus (Main)

R. Nicer (Neckar)

AGRI DECUMATES

R. Rhenus (Rhine)

R. Rhenus (Rhine)

Augusta Raurica

Vindonissa

Lake Constance

LOWER GERMANY

RAETIA

The Rhenus (Rhine) became the Roman frontier in Julius Caesar's time, though shortlived attempts were made to advance the boundary to the Albis (Elbe) by Augustus (until Varus' disaster in the Teutoburg Forest in A.D. 9) and Tiberius (under his nephew Germanicus, A.D. 14-17). The Agri Decumates, in the reentrant between the Upper Rhine and Upper Danube, were occupied under Vespasian (69-79) and Domitian (81-96) – in whose reign the military regions of Upper and Lower Germany were converted into provinces – and Antoninus Pius (138-161) pushed the frontier some miles forward, constructing new defences. But the Agri were evacuated by Gallienus (c.259-260).

0   100
Miles

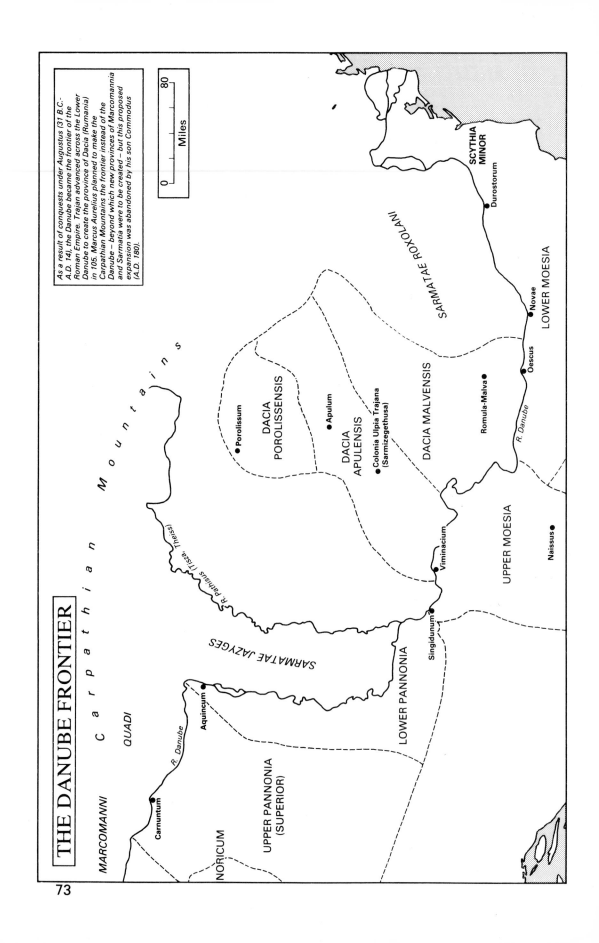

THE DANUBE FRONTIER

As a result of conquests under Augustus (31 B.C.–A.D. 14), the Danube became the frontier of the Roman Empire. Trajan advanced across the Lower Danube to create the province of Dacia (Rumania) in 105. Marcus Aurelius planned to make the Carpathian Mountains the frontier instead of the Danube – beyond which new provinces of Marcomannia and Sarmatia were to be created – but this proposed expansion was abandoned by his son Commodus (A.D. 180).

MARCOMANNI

C a r p a t h i a n   M o u n t a i n s

QUADI

NORICUM

UPPER PANNONIA (SUPERIOR)

R. Danube

Carnuntum ●

Aquincum ●

R. Parhisus (Tisza / Theiss)

SARMATAE JAZYGES

LOWER PANNONIA

Singidunum ●

Viminacium ●

UPPER MOESIA

Naissus ●

DACIA POROLISSENSIS

● Porolissum

DACIA APULENSIS

● Apulum

● Colonia Ulpia Trajana (Sarmizegethusa)

DACIA MALVENSIS

Romula-Malva ●

SARMATAE ROXOLANI

R. Danube

Oescus ●

Novae ●

LOWER MOESIA

Durostorum ●

SCYTHIA MINOR

Miles

0   80

73

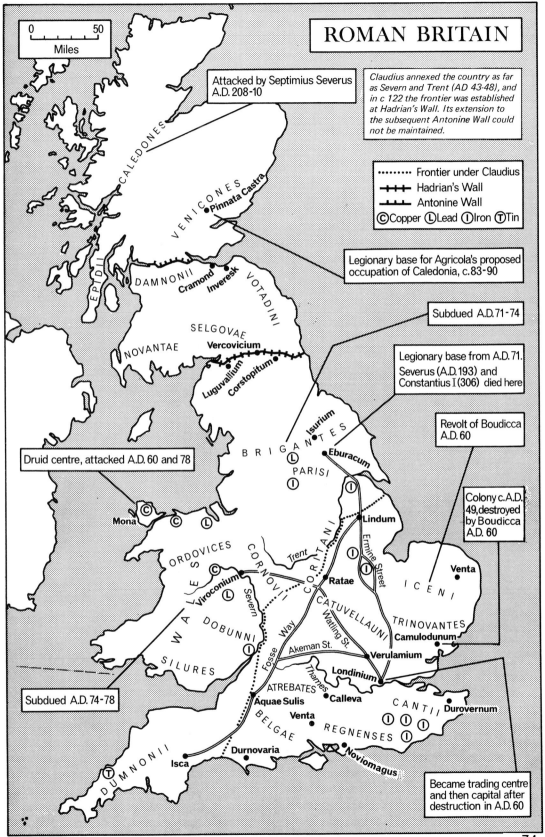

ROMAN BRITAIN

0 — 50 Miles

Claudius annexed the country as far
as Severn and Trent (AD 43-48), and
in c 122 the frontier was established
at Hadrian's Wall. Its extension to
the subsequent Antonine Wall could
not be maintained.

········· Frontier under Claudius
—+++— Hadrian's Wall
—+++— Antonine Wall
ⒸCopper ⓁLead ⒾIron ⓉTin

Attacked by Septimius Severus
A.D. 208-10

Legionary base for Agricola's proposed
occupation of Caledonia, c.83-90

Subdued A.D. 71-74

Legionary base from A.D.71.
Severus (A.D.193) and
Constantius I (306) died here

Druid centre, attacked A.D. 60 and 78

Revolt of Boudicca
A.D. 60

Colony c.A.D.
49, destroyed
by Boudicca
A.D. 60

Subdued A.D. 74-78

Became trading centre
and then capital after
destruction in A.D. 60

CALEDONES
VENICONES
Pinnata Castra
EPIDII
DAMNONII
Cramond   **Inveresk**
VOTADINI
SELGOVAE
Vercovicium
NOVANTAE
Luguvallium   **Corstopitum**
BRIGANTES
Isurium
Ⓛ **Eburacum**
PARISI
Ⓘ
Ⓒ
Mona   Ⓒ   Ⓛ
ORDOVICES
Ⓒ
CORNOVII
Ⓘ **Lindum**
Ermine Street
Ⓘ
Ⓘ
Venta
CORITANI
Trent
Ratae
W A L E S
Viroconium
Ⓛ
Severn
ICENI
CATUVELLAUNI
DOBUNNI
TRINOVANTES
Ⓘ
Fosse Way
Akeman St.
Watling St.
Camulodunum
SILURES
Verulamium
Thames
Londinium
ATREBATES
Aqua Sulis   **Calleva**
CANTII
Durovernum
Venta
BELGAE   REGNENSES   Ⓘ Ⓘ Ⓘ
Ⓣ
DUMNONII   **Durnovaria**
Isca   **Noviomagus**

74

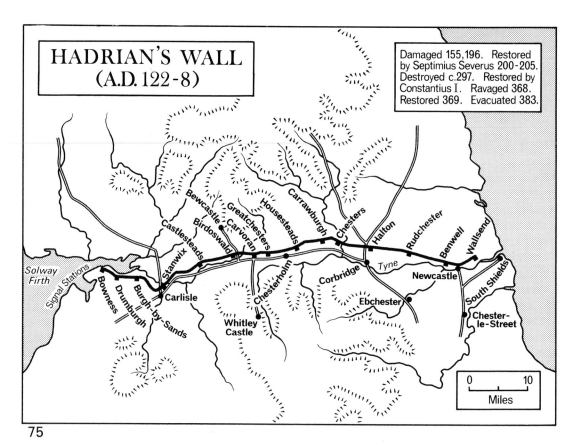

HADRIAN'S WALL
(A.D. 122-8)

Damaged 155, 196. Restored by Septimius Severus 200-205. Destroyed c.297. Restored by Constantius I. Ravaged 368. Restored 369. Evacuated 383.

Bewcastle
Greatchesters
Carvoran
Birdoswald
Castlesteads
Carrawburgh
Housesteads
Chesters
Halton
Rudchester
Benwell
Wallsend

Stanwix
Chesterholm
Corbridge
Tyne
Newcastle

Solway Firth
Signal Stations
Bowness
Drumburgh
Burgh-by-Sands
Carlisle
Ebchester
South Shields

Whitley Castle
Chester-le-Street

0   10
Miles

75

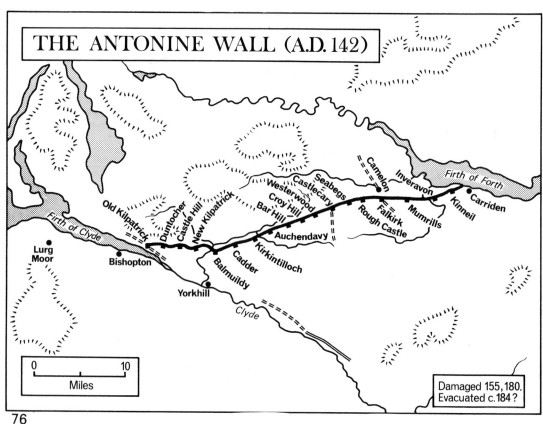

THE ANTONINE WALL (A.D. 142)

Camelon
Inveravon
Firth of Forth
Seabegs
Castlecary
Westerwood
Croy Hill
Bar Hill
Falkirk
Mumrills
Kinneil
Carriden
Rough Castle

Old Kilpatrick
Duntocher
Castle Hill
New Kilpatrick
Auchendavy

Firth of Clyde

Lurg Moor
Bishopton
Cadder
Balmuildy
Kirkintilloch
Yorkhill
Clyde

0   10
Miles

Damaged 155, 180. Evacuated c.184?

76

THE WORLD ACCORDING TO PTOLEMY, c. A.D. 150

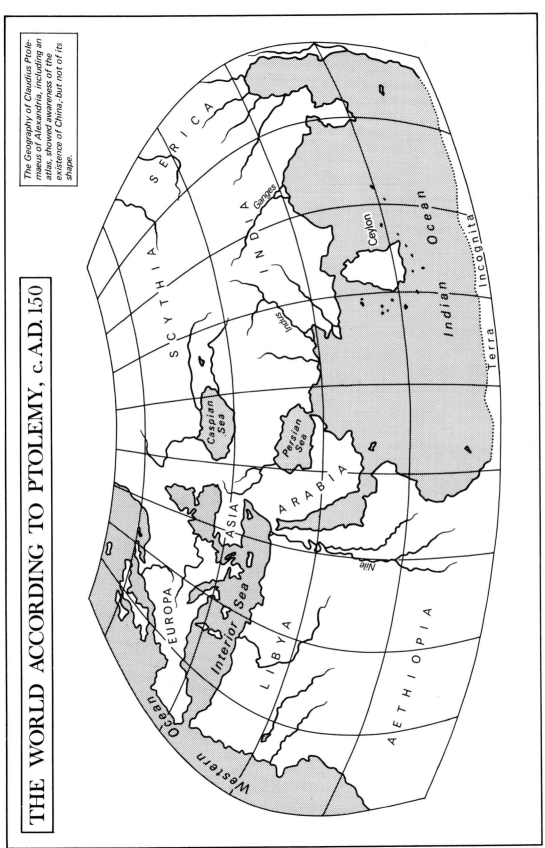

The Geography of Claudius Ptole-maeus of Alexandria, including an atlas, showed awareness of the existence of China, but not of its shape.

SERICA

SCYTHIA

INDIA

Ganges

Indus

Caspian Sea

Persian Sea

ARABIA

ASIA

EUROPA

Interior Sea

LIBYA

Nile

AETHIOPIA

Western Ocean

Ceylon

Indian Ocean

Terra Incognita

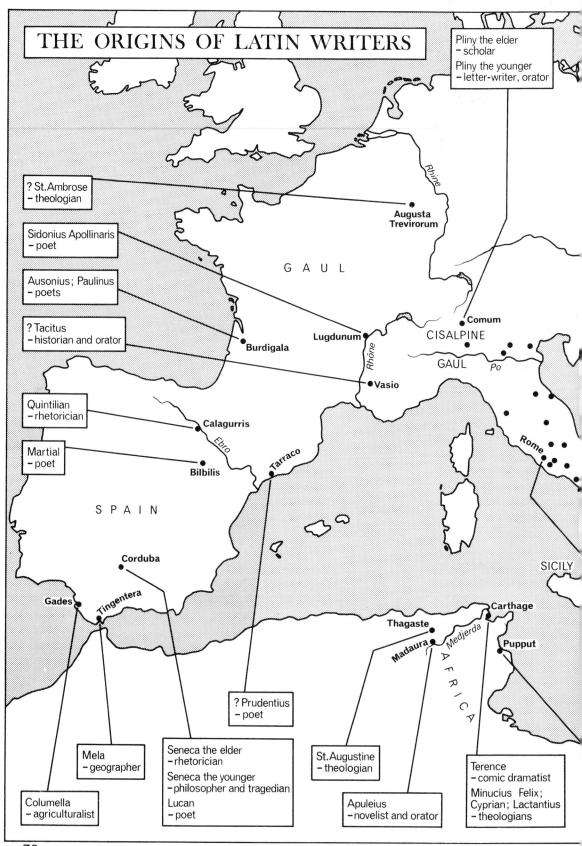

THE ORIGINS OF LATIN WRITERS

Pliny the elder
– scholar
Pliny the younger
– letter-writer, orator

? St.Ambrose
– theologian

Sidonius Apollinaris
– poet

Ausonius; Paulinus
– poets

? Tacitus
– historian and orator

Quintilian
– rhetorician

Martial
– poet

Mela
– geographer

Columella
– agriculturalist

Seneca the elder
– rhetorician
Seneca the younger
– philosopher and tragedian
Lucan
– poet

? Prudentius
– poet

St.Augustine
– theologian

Apuleius
– novelist and orator

Terence
– comic dramatist
Minucius Felix;
Cyprian; Lactantius
– theologians

GAUL

Augusta
Trevirorum

Rhine

Comum

CISALPINE

GAUL   Po

Lugdunum

Rhône

Burdigala

Vasio

Calagurris

Ebro

Tarraco

Rome

Bilbilis

SPAIN

SICILY

Corduba

Gades

Tingentera

Thagaste

Carthage

Madaura   Medjerda

Pupput

AFRICA

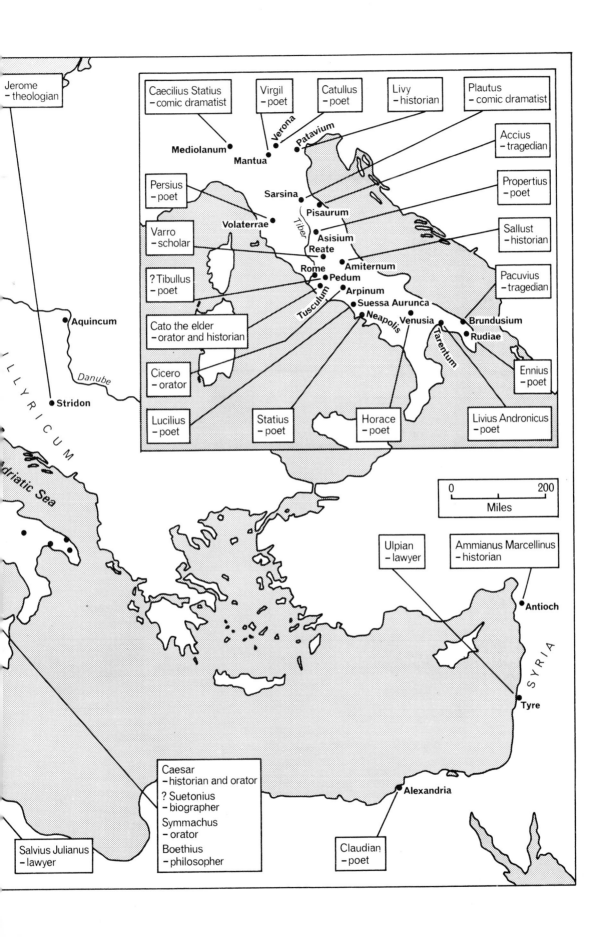

Jerome
– theologian

Caecilius Statius
– comic dramatist

Virgil
– poet

Catullus
– poet

Livy
– historian

Plautus
– comic dramatist

Accius
– tragedian

Propertius
– poet

Sallust
– historian

Pacuvius
– tragedian

Persius
– poet

Varro
– scholar

?Tibullus
– poet

Cato the elder
– orator and historian

Cicero
– orator

Lucilius
– poet

Statius
– poet

Horace
– poet

Livius Andronicus
– poet

Ennius
– poet

Mediolanum

Mantua

Verona

Patavium

Sarsina

Pisaurum

Volaterrae

Tiber

Asisium

Reate

Rome

Amiternum

Pedum

Arpinum

Tusculum

Suessa Aurunca

Neapolis

Venusia

Brundusium

Rudiae

Tarentum

Aquincum

ILLYRICUM

Danube

Stridon

Adriatic Sea

0   200
Miles

Ulpian
– lawyer

Ammianus Marcellinus
– historian

Antioch

SYRIA

Tyre

Salvius Julianus
– lawyer

Caesar
– historian and orator

?Suetonius
– biographer

Symmachus
– orator

Boethius
– philosopher

Alexandria

Claudian
– poet

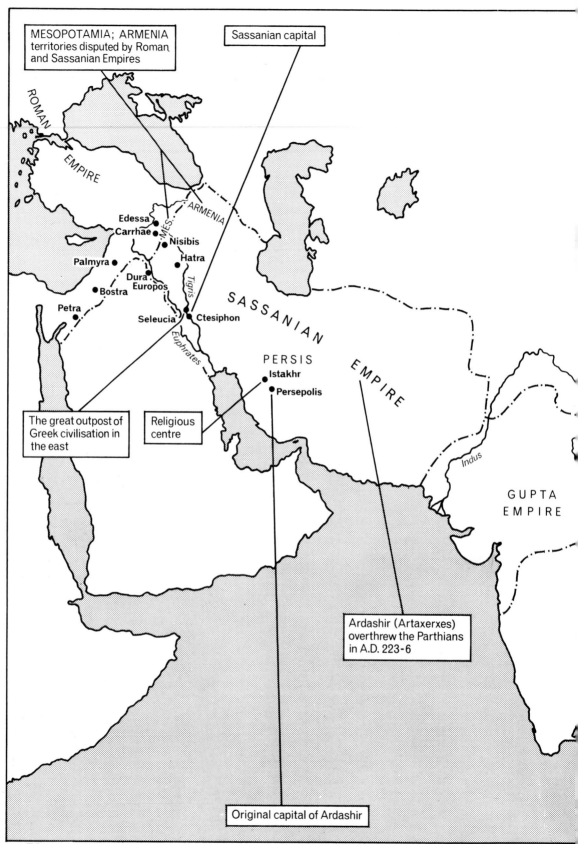

MESOPOTAMIA; ARMENIA
territories disputed by Roman
and Sassanian Empires

Sassanian capital

ROMAN

EMPIRE

ARMENIA

Edessa
Carrhae
MES.
Nisibis
Hatra
Palmyra
Dura
Europos
Bostra
Tigris
Petra
Seleucia
Ctesiphon
Euphrates

SASSANIAN

EMPIRE

PERSIS
Istakhr
Persepolis

The great outpost of
Greek civilisation in
the east

Religious
centre

Indus

GUPTA
EMPIRE

Ardashir (Artaxerxes)
overthrew the Parthians
in A.D. 223-6

Original capital of Ardashir

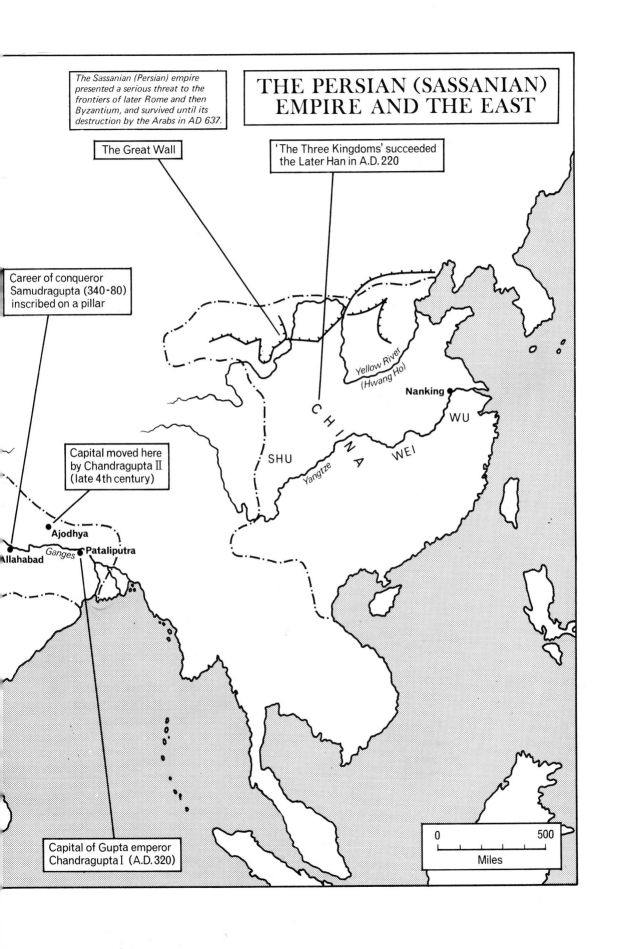

THE PERSIAN (SASSANIAN) EMPIRE AND THE EAST

The Sassanian (Persian) empire presented a serious threat to the frontiers of later Rome and then Byzantium, and survived until its destruction by the Arabs in AD 637.

The Great Wall

'The Three Kingdoms' succeeded the Later Han in A.D. 220

Career of conqueror Samudragupta (340-80) inscribed on a pillar

Yellow River (Hwang Ho)

Nanking

C H I N A

WU

SHU

WEI

Yangtze

Capital moved here by Chandragupta II (late 4th century)

Ajodhya

Ganges **Pataliputra**

Allahabad

Capital of Gupta emperor Chandragupta I (A.D. 320)

0 — 500
Miles

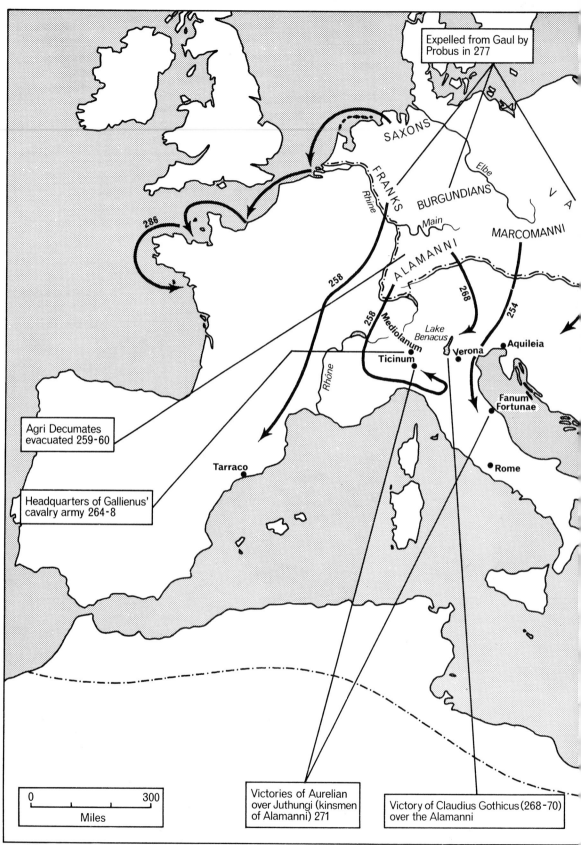

Expelled from Gaul by
Probus in 277

SAXONS

FRANKS

BURGUNDIANS

MARCOMANNI

Elbe

Rhine

Main

ALAMANNI

286

258

258

268

254

258

Mediolanum

Lake
Benacus

Verona

Aquileia

Ticinum

Rhône

Fanum
Fortunae

Agri Decumates
evacuated 259-60

Tarraco

Rome

Headquarters of Gallienus'
cavalry army 264-8

0   300

Miles

Victories of Aurelian
over Juthungi (kinsmen
of Alamanni) 271

Victory of Claudius Gothicus (268-70)
over the Alamanni

GERMAN INVASIONS IN THE THIRD CENTURY A.D.

From the 230s until the 260s the Germans burst over the frontiers with ever increasing force, but then the dissolution of the empire was prevented by Gallienus, Claudius II Gothicus, Aurelian and Probus.

Evacuated c. 271

First crossed the Danube under Severus Alexander (222-35)

King lends fleet to raiders 254

Decius fell to Goths 251

Dnieper

Dniester

EAST GOTHS

HERULI

A L S

Aquincum

DACIA

Cimmerian Bosphorus

Panticapaeum

WEST GOTHS

Danube

Abrittus

264

269

Marcianopolis

Black Sea

BITHYNIA

Trapezus

SASSANIAN

EMPIRE

Naïssus

Philippopolis

Byzantium

Chalcedon

Thessalonica

Pessinus

Ephesus

Sparta

Overrun by Goths 256

Victory of Gallienus over Goths 268

Captured by Goths from Decius (249-51)

Sacked by Goths in 253

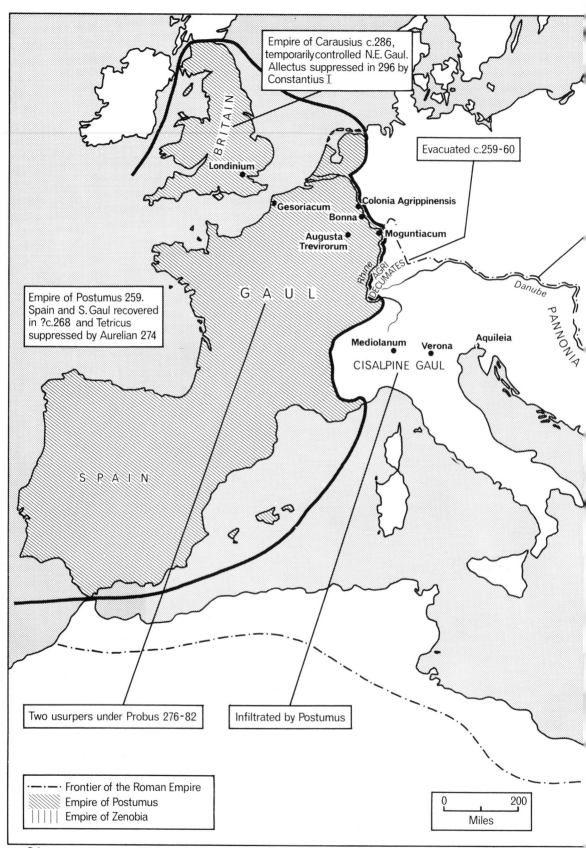

Empire of Carausius c.286, temporarily controlled N.E. Gaul. Allectus suppressed in 296 by Constantius I

Evacuated c.259-60

Empire of Postumus 259. Spain and S. Gaul recovered in ?c.268 and Tetricus suppressed by Aurelian 274

Londinium

BRITAIN

Colonia Agrippinensis

Gesoriacum

Bonna

Augusta Trevirorum

Moguntiacum

Rhine

AGRI DECUMATES

Danube

PANNONIA

G A U L

Mediolanum

Verona

Aquileia

CISALPINE GAUL

S P A I N

Two usurpers under Probus 276-82

Infiltrated by Postumus

- · - · - Frontier of the Roman Empire
  Empire of Postumus
  Empire of Zenobia

0   200
    Miles

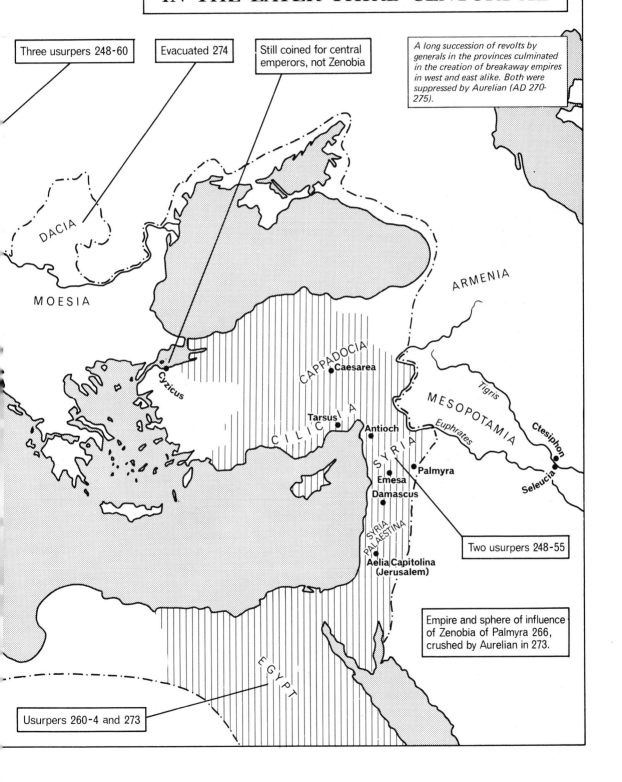

THE BREAKDOWN AND RECOVERY
OF THE ROMAN EMPIRE
IN THE LATER THIRD CENTURY A.D.

Three usurpers 248-60

Evacuated 274

Still coined for central emperors, not Zenobia

A long succession of revolts by generals in the provinces culminated in the creation of breakaway empires in west and east alike. Both were suppressed by Aurelian (AD 270-275).

DACIA

MOESIA

ARMENIA

CAPPADOCIA
● Caesarea

Tigris

MESOPOTAMIA

Ctesiphon ●

Cyzicus ●

Tarsus ●

C I L I C I A

Antioch ●

Euphrates

S Y R I A

● Palmyra

Seleucia ●

Emesa ●
Damascus ●

SYRIA
PALAESTINA

Two usurpers 248-55

Aelia Capitolina
(Jerusalem) ●

Empire and sphere of influence of Zenobia of Palmyra 266, crushed by Aurelian in 273.

E G Y P T

Usurpers 260-4 and 273

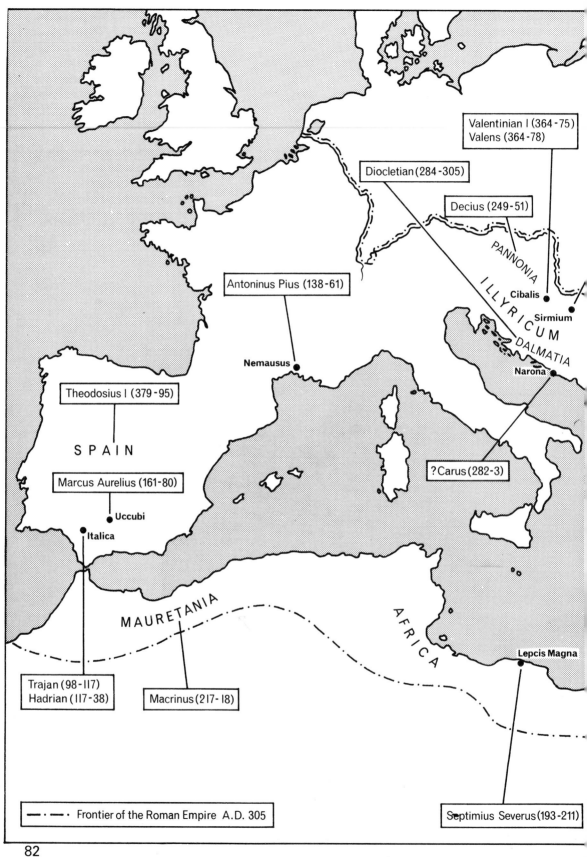

Valentinian I (364-75)
Valens (364-78)

Diocletian (284-305)

Decius (249-51)

PANNONIA

ILLYRICUM

Cibalis

Sirmium

Antoninus Pius (138-61)

DALMATIA

Narona

Nemausus

Theodosius I (379-95)

SPAIN

?Carus (282-3)

Marcus Aurelius (161-80)

Uccubi

Italica

MAURETANIA

AFRICA

Lepcis Magna

Trajan (98-117)
Hadrian (117-38)

Macrinus (217-18)

—·—·— Frontier of the Roman Empire A.D. 305

Septimius Severus (193-211)

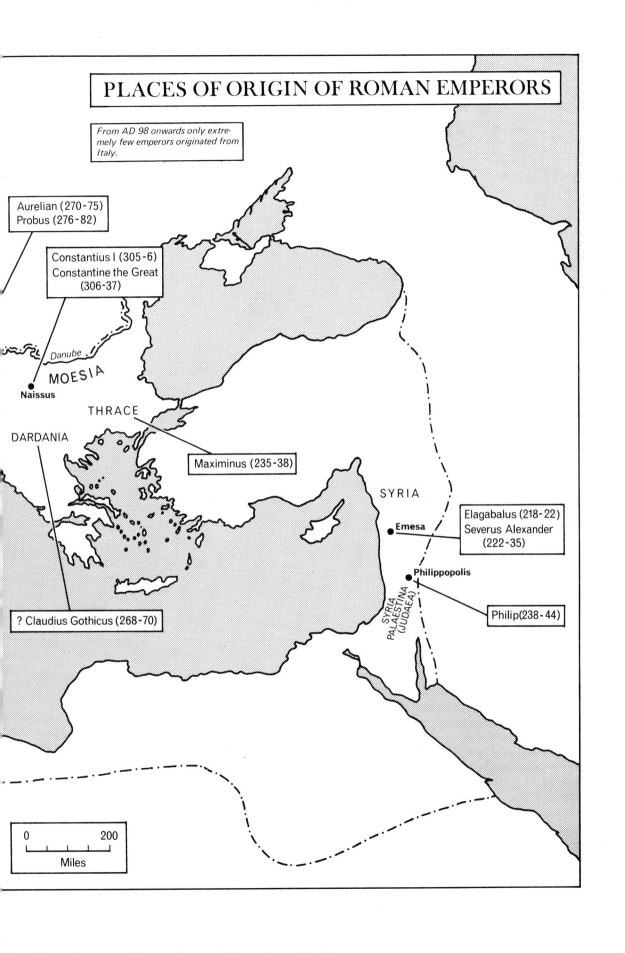

PLACES OF ORIGIN OF ROMAN EMPERORS

From AD 98 onwards only extremely few emperors originated from Italy.

Aurelian (270-75)
Probus (276-82)

Constantius I (305-6)
Constantine the Great
(306-37)

Danube

MOESIA

● **Naissus**

THRACE

DARDANIA

Maximinus (235-38)

SYRIA

● **Emesa**

Elagabalus (218-22)
Severus Alexander
(222-35)

● **Philippopolis**

SYRIA
PALAESTINA
(JUDAEA)

Philip(238-44)

? Claudius Gothicus (268-70)

0   200

Miles

Jews deported from
Rome by Tiberius
A.D. 14 - 37

Areas of widespread Jewish settlement

Towns with large Jewish communities

83

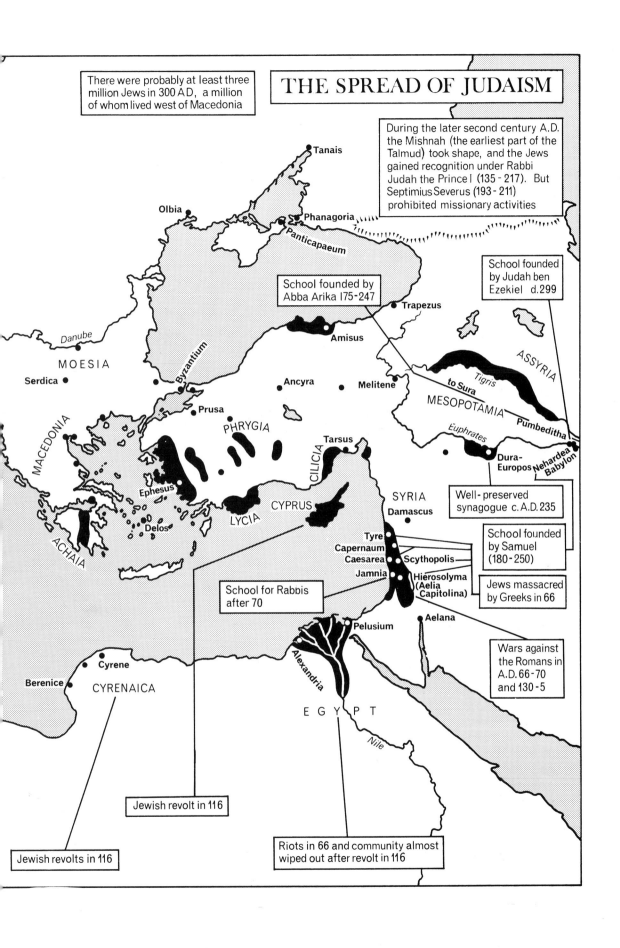

THE SPREAD OF JUDAISM

There were probably at least three million Jews in 300 A.D., a million of whom lived west of Macedonia

During the later second century A.D. the Mishnah (the earliest part of the Talmud) took shape, and the Jews gained recognition under Rabbi Judah the Prince I (135 - 217). But Septimius Severus (193 - 211) prohibited missionary activities

Tanais

Olbia

Phanagoria

Panticapaeum

School founded by Abba Arika 175-247

Trapezus

School founded by Judah ben Ezekiel d.299

Danube

MOESIA

Serdica

Byzantium

Amisus

ASSYRIA

Tigris

to Sura

MESOPOTAMIA

Ancyra

Melitene

Pumbeditha

Prusa

Euphrates

MACEDONIA

PHRYGIA

Dura-Europos

Nehardea

Babylon

Tarsus

CILICIA

Ephesus

CYPRUS

SYRIA

Well-preserved synagogue c. A.D. 235

LYCIA

Damascus

Delos

ACHAIA

Tyre
Capernaum
Caesarea

School founded by Samuel (180-250)

Scythopolis

Jamnia

Hierosolyma (Aelia Capitolina)

Jews massacred by Greeks in 66

School for Rabbis after 70

Aelana

Pelusium

Wars against the Romans in A.D. 66-70 and 130-5

Cyrene

Alexandria

Berenice

CYRENAICA

E G Y P T

Nile

Jewish revolt in 116

Jewish revolts in 116

Riots in 66 and community almost wiped out after revolt in 116

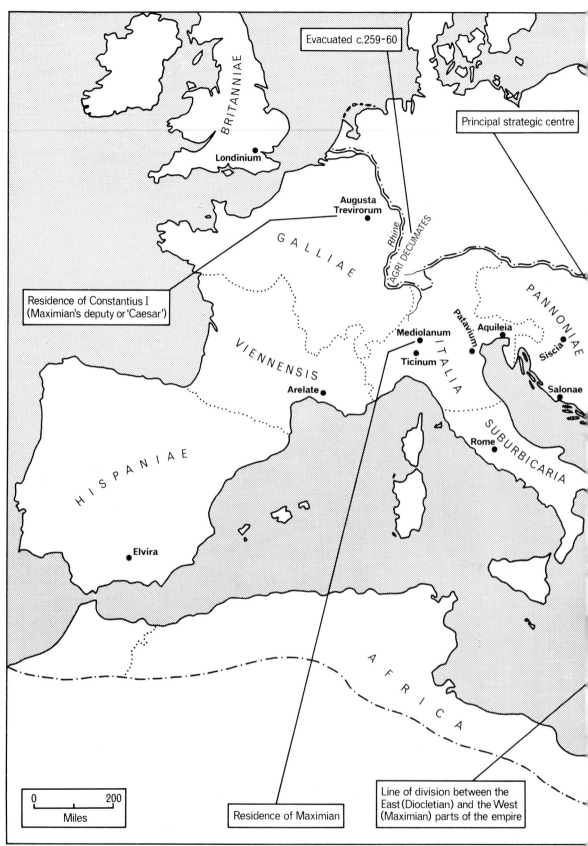

Evacuated c.259-60

Principal strategic centre

BRITANNIAE

Londinium

Augusta
Trevirorum

GALLIAE

Rhine

AGRI DECUMATES

PANNONIAE

Residence of Constantius I
(Maximian's deputy or 'Caesar')

VIENNENSIS

Mediolanum

Ticinum

Patavium

Aquileia

Siscia

ITALIA

Salonae

Arelate

HISPANIAE

Rome

SUBURBICARIA

Elvira

AFRICA

0   200
Miles

Residence of Maximian

Line of division between the
East (Diocletian) and the West
(Maximian) parts of the empire

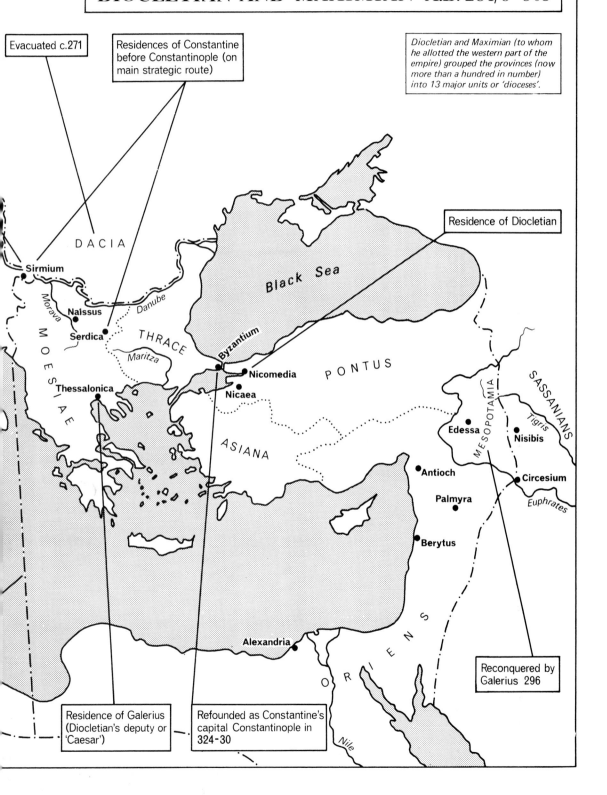

THE ROMAN EMPIRE UNDER
DIOCLETIAN AND MAXIMIAN A.D. 284/6-305

Evacuated c.271

Residences of Constantine
before Constantinople (on
main strategic route)

*Diocletian and Maximian (to whom
he allotted the western part of the
empire) grouped the provinces (now
more than a hundred in number)
into 13 major units or 'dioceses'.*

Residence of Diocletian

DACIA

Sirmium

Morava

Naissus

Danube

Serdica

THRACE

Maritza

Black Sea

Byzantium

Nicomedia

PONTUS

MOESIAE

Thessalonica

Nicaea

SASSANIANS

MESOPOTAMIA

Tigris

Edessa

Nisibis

ASIANA

Antioch

Circesium

Palmyra

Euphrates

Berytus

O   R   I   E   N   S

Alexandria

Reconquered by
Galerius 296

Residence of Galerius
(Diocletian's deputy or
'Caesar')

Refounded as Constantine's
capital Constantinople in
324-30

Nile

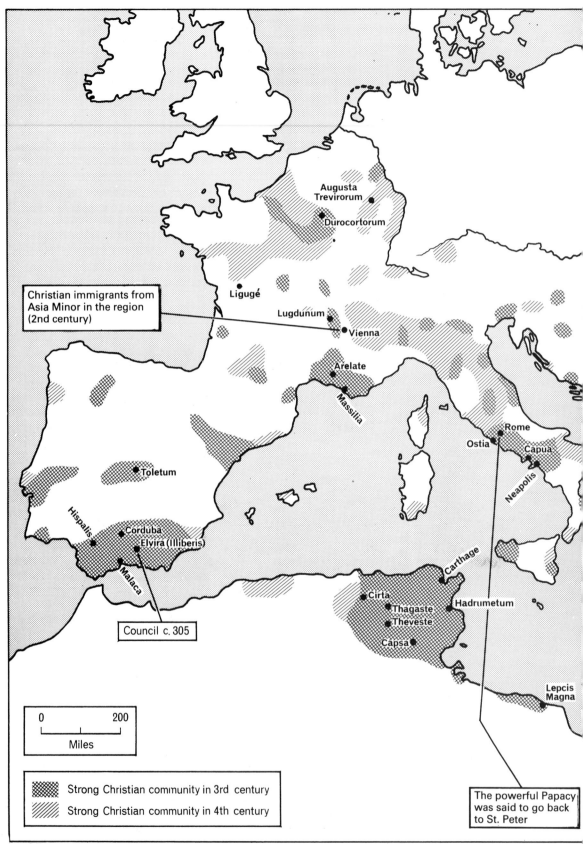

Christian immigrants from
Asia Minor in the region
(2nd century)

Council c. 305

The powerful Papacy
was said to go back
to St. Peter

Augusta
Trevirorum

Durocortorum

Ligugé

Lugdunum

Vienna

Arelate

Massilia

Rome

Ostia

Capua

Neapolis

Toletum

Hispalis

Corduba

Elvira (Illiberis)

Malaca

Carthage

Cirta

Thagaste

Hadrumetum

Theveste

Capsa

Lepcis
Magna

0   200
Miles

Strong Christian community in 3rd century

Strong Christian community in 4th century

THE SPREAD OF CHRISTIANITY

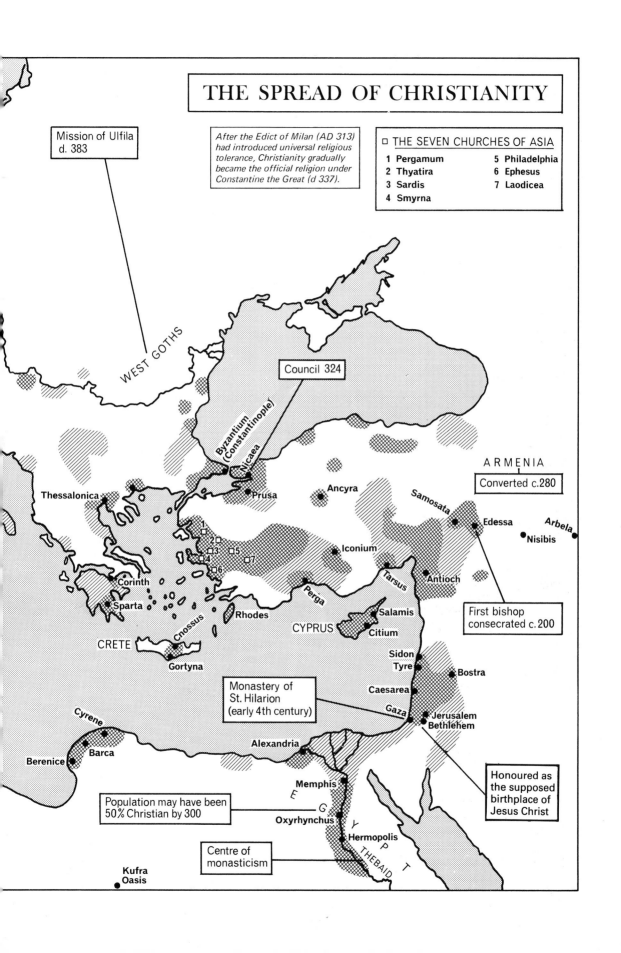

Mission of Ulfila
d. 383

After the Edict of Milan (AD 313)
had introduced universal religious
tolerance, Christianity gradually
became the official religion under
Constantine the Great (d 337).

☐ THE SEVEN CHURCHES OF ASIA

1 Pergamum   **5** Philadelphia
2 Thyatira   **6** Ephesus
3 Sardis   **7** Laodicea
4 Smyrna

WEST GOTHS

Council 324

Byzantium
(Constantinople)
Nicaea

ARMENIA
Converted c.280

Thessalonica

Ancyra

Prusa

Samosata

Edessa

Arbela

Nisibis

☐2
☐3   ☐5
☐4   ☐7
☐6

Iconium

Corinth

Sparta

Rhodes

Perga

Tarsus

Antioch

First bishop
consecrated c.200

Cnossus

CRETE

Gortyna

Salamis

CYPRUS

Citium

Sidon
Tyre

Bostra

Caesarea

Monastery of
St. Hilarion
(early 4th century)

Gaza

Jerusalem
Bethlehem

Cyrene

Barca

Honoured as
the supposed
birthplace of
Jesus Christ

Berenice

Alexandria

Memphis

E

Population may have been
50% Christian by 300

G

Y

Oxyrhynchus

P

Centre of
monasticism

Hermopolis

T

THEBAID

Kufra
Oasis

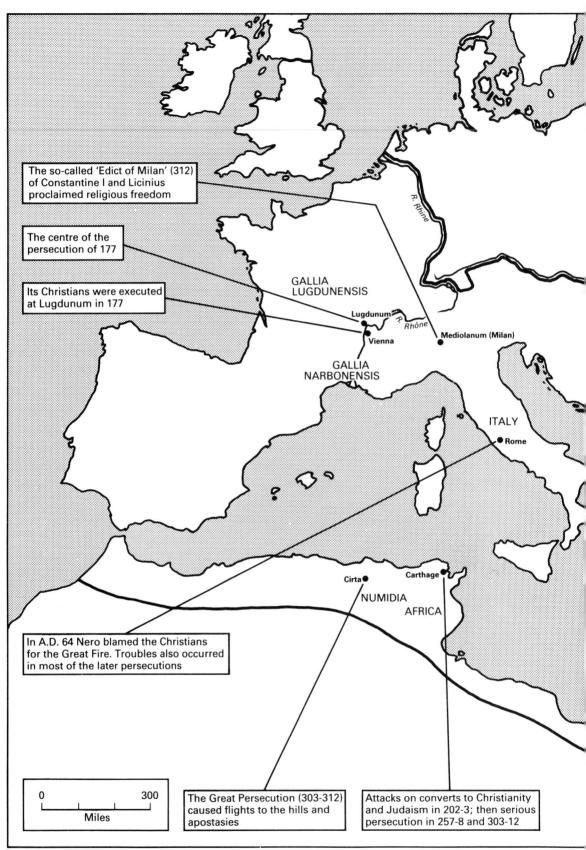

The so-called 'Edict of Milan' (312)
of Constantine I and Licinius
proclaimed religious freedom

The centre of the
persecution of 177

Its Christians were executed
at Lugdunum in 177

GALLIA
LUGDUNENSIS

R. Rhine

Lugdunum
R. Rhône

Vienna

Mediolanum (Milan)

GALLIA
NARBONENSIS

ITALY

Rome

Cirta

Carthage

NUMIDIA

AFRICA

In A.D. 64 Nero blamed the Christians
for the Great Fire. Troubles also occurred
in most of the later persecutions

0   300

Miles

The Great Persecution (303-312)
caused flights to the hills and
apostasies

Attacks on converts to Christianity
and Judaism in 202-3; then serious
persecution in 257-8 and 303-12

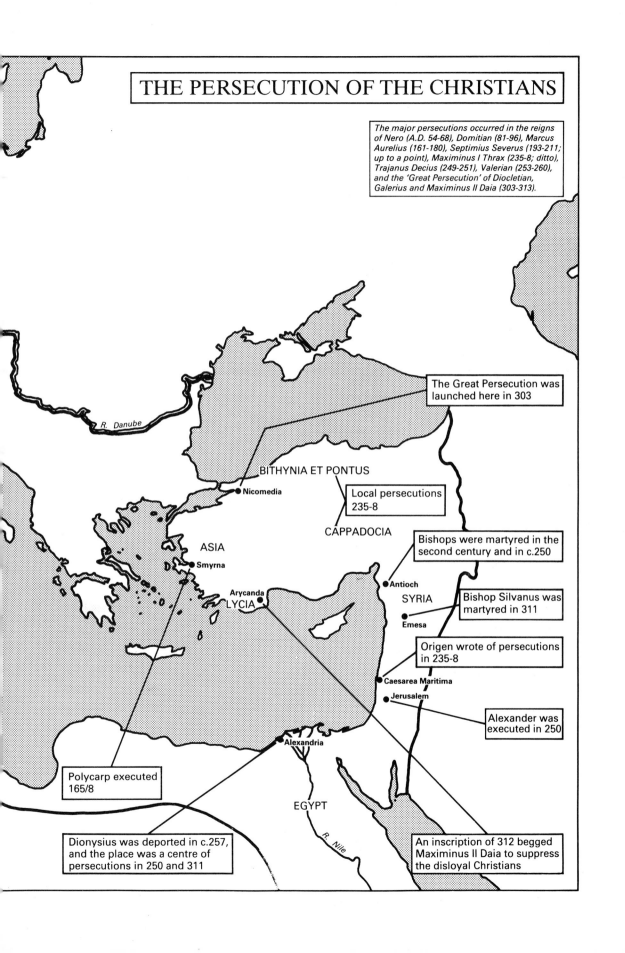

THE PERSECUTION OF THE CHRISTIANS

The major persecutions occurred in the reigns of Nero (A.D. 54-68), Domitian (81-96), Marcus Aurelius (161-180), Septimius Severus (193-211; up to a point), Maximinus I Thrax (235-8; ditto), Trajanus Decius (249-251), Valerian (253-260), and the 'Great Persecution' of Diocletian, Galerius and Maximinus II Daia (303-313).

R. Danube

The Great Persecution was launched here in 303

BITHYNIA ET PONTUS

● Nicomedia

Local persecutions 235-8

CAPPADOCIA

Bishops were martyred in the second century and in c.250

ASIA

● Smyrna

● Antioch

SYRIA

Bishop Silvanus was martyred in 311

Arycanda
LYCIA

● Emesa

Origen wrote of persecutions in 235-8

● Caesarea Maritima

● Jerusalem

Alexander was executed in 250

● Alexandria

Polycarp executed 165/8

EGYPT

An inscription of 312 begged Maximinus II Daia to suppress the disloyal Christians

Dionysius was deported in c.257, and the place was a centre of persecutions in 250 and 311

R. Nile

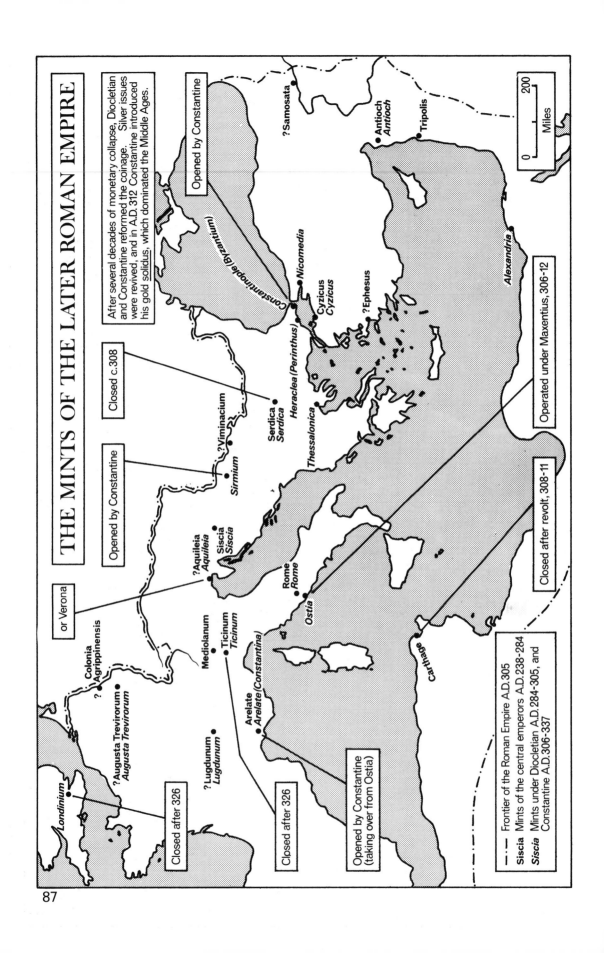

THE MINTS OF THE LATER ROMAN EMPIRE

After several decades of monetary collapse, Diocletian and Constantine reformed the coinage. Silver issues were revived, and in A.D. 312 Constantine introduced his gold solidus, which dominated the Middle Ages.

Opened by Constantine

Closed c.308

Opened by Constantine

or Verona

Colonia Agrippinensis

?

?Augusta Trevirorum
Augusta Trevirorum

Londinium

Closed after 326

?Lugdunum
Lugdunum

Closed after 326

Mediolanum

Ticinum
Ticinum

Arelate
Arelate (Constantina)

Opened by Constantine
(taking over from Ostia)

?Aquileia
Aquileia

Siscia
Siscia

Rome
Rome

Ostia

Carthage

?Viminacium

Sirmium

Serdica
Serdica

Thessalonica

Constantinople (Byzantium)

Heraclea (Perinthus)

Nicomedia

Cyzicus
Cyzicus

?Ephesus

?Samosata

Antioch
Antioch

Tripolis

Alexandria

Operated under Maxentius, 306-12

Closed after revolt, 308-11

—·— Frontier of the Roman Empire A.D. 305

Siscia Mints of the central emperors A.D. 238-284

Siscia Mints under Diocletian A.D. 284-305, and Constantine A.D. 306-337

0   200
Miles

87

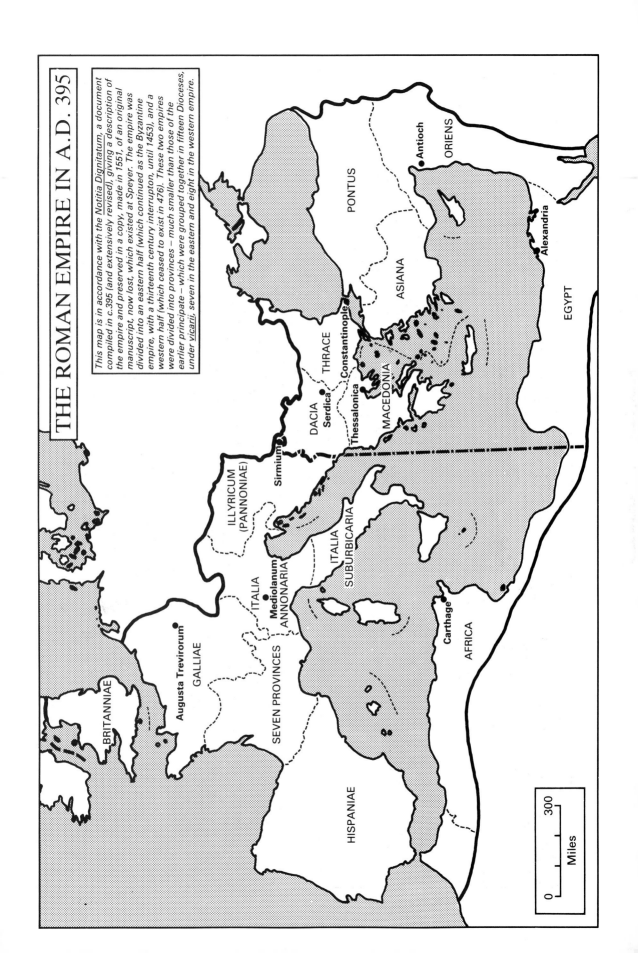

THE ROMAN EMPIRE IN A.D. 395

This map is in accordance with the *Notitia Dignitatum*, a document compiled in c.395 (and extensively revised), giving a description of the empire and preserved in a copy, made in 1551, of an original manuscript, now lost, which existed at Speyer. The empire was divided into an eastern half (which continued as the Byzantine empire, with a thirteenth century interruption, until 1453), and a western half (which ceased to exist in 476). These two empires were divided into provinces – much smaller than those of the earlier principate – which were grouped together in fifteen Dioceses, under *vicarii* seven in the eastern and eight in the western empire.

ORIENS

Antioch

PONTUS

ASIANA

Alexandria

EGYPT

THRACE

Constantinople

DACIA

Serdica

Thessalonica

MACEDONIA

Sirmium

ILLYRICUM
(PANNONIAE)

ITALIA

SUBURBICARIA

ITALIA
ANNONARIA

Mediolanum

AFRICA

Carthage

BRITANNIAE

Augusta Trevirorum

GALLIAE

SEVEN PROVINCES

HISPANIAE

0   300

Miles

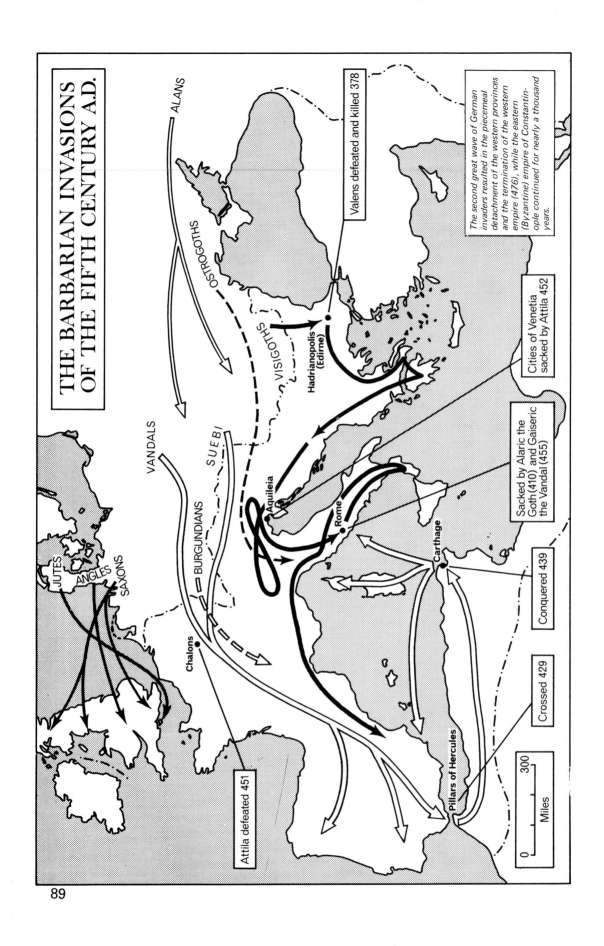

THE BARBARIAN INVASIONS
OF THE FIFTH CENTURY A.D.

ALANS

OSTROGOTHS

VISIGOTHS

Valens defeated and killed 378

The second great wave of German
invaders resulted in the piecemeal
detachment of the western provinces
and the termination of the western
empire (476), while the eastern
(Byzantine) empire of Constantinople continued for nearly a thousand
years.

Cities of Venetia
sacked by Attila 452

Hadrianopolis
(Edirne)

VANDALS

SUEBI

BURGUNDIANS

Aquileia

Rome

Sacked by Alaric the
Goth (410) and Gaiseric
the Vandal (455)

JUTES

ANGLES

SAXONS

Chalons

Carthage

Conquered 439

Attila defeated 451

Pillars of Hercules

Crossed 429

300

0

Miles

89

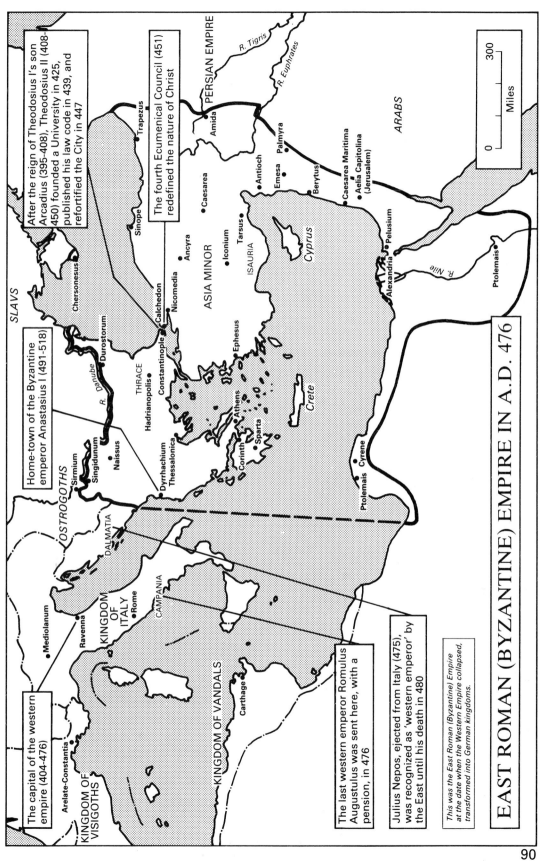

After the reign of Theodosius I's son Arcadius (395-408), Theodosius II (408-450) founded a University in 425, published his law code in 439, and refortified the City in 447

The fourth Ecumenical Council (451) redefined the nature of Christ

PERSIAN EMPIRE

R. Tigris

R. Euphrates

Trapezus

Amida

Palmyra

ARABS

Caesarea

Antioch

Emesa

Berytus

Caesarea Maritima

Sinope

Aelia Capitolina
(Jerusalem)

Nicomedia

Ancyra

Iconium

Tarsus

Cyprus

ASIA MINOR

ISAURIA

Alexandria

Pelusium

Calchedon

R. Nile

Ptolemais

Chersonesus

Constantinople

Ephesus

Home-town of the Byzantine emperor Anastasius I (491-518)

SLAVS

Durostorum

R. Danube

THRACE

Hadrianopolis

Crete

Sirmium

Singidunum

Naissus

Dyrrhachium

Thessalonica

Athens

Corinth

Sparta

OSTROGOTHS

Cyrene

Ptolemais

The capital of the western empire (404-476)

Arelate-Constantia

KINGDOM OF VISIGOTHS

Mediolanum

Ravenna

DALMATIA

KINGDOM
OF
ITALY

Rome

CAMPANIA

KINGDOM OF VANDALS

Carthage

The last western emperor Romulus Augustulus was sent here, with a pension, in 476

Julius Nepos, ejected from Italy (475), was recognized as 'western emperor' by the East until his death in 480

This was the East Roman (Byzantine) Empire at the date when the Western Empire collapsed, transformed into German kingdoms.

0   300
Miles

EAST ROMAN (BYZANTINE) EMPIRE IN A.D. 476

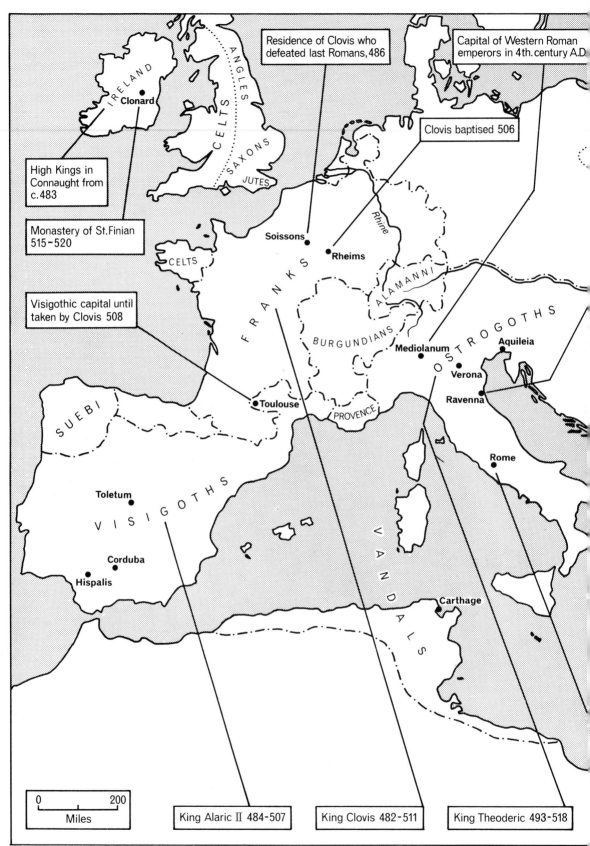

Residence of Clovis who
defeated last Romans, 486

Capital of Western Roman
emperors in 4th. century A.D.

Clovis baptised 506

High Kings in
Connaught from
c. 483

Monastery of St. Finian
515–520

Visigothic capital until
taken by Clovis 508

IRELAND

Clonard

CELTS

ANGLES

SAXONS

JUTES

CELTS

FRANKS

Soissons

Rheims

Rhine

ALAMANNI

OSTROGOTHS

BURGUNDIANS

Mediolanum

Aquileia

Verona

Ravenna

Toulouse

PROVENCE

SUEBI

Rome

Toletum

VISIGOTHS

VANDALS

Corduba

Hispalis

Carthage

0	200

Miles

King Alaric Ⅱ 484–507

King Clovis 482–511

King Theoderic 493–518

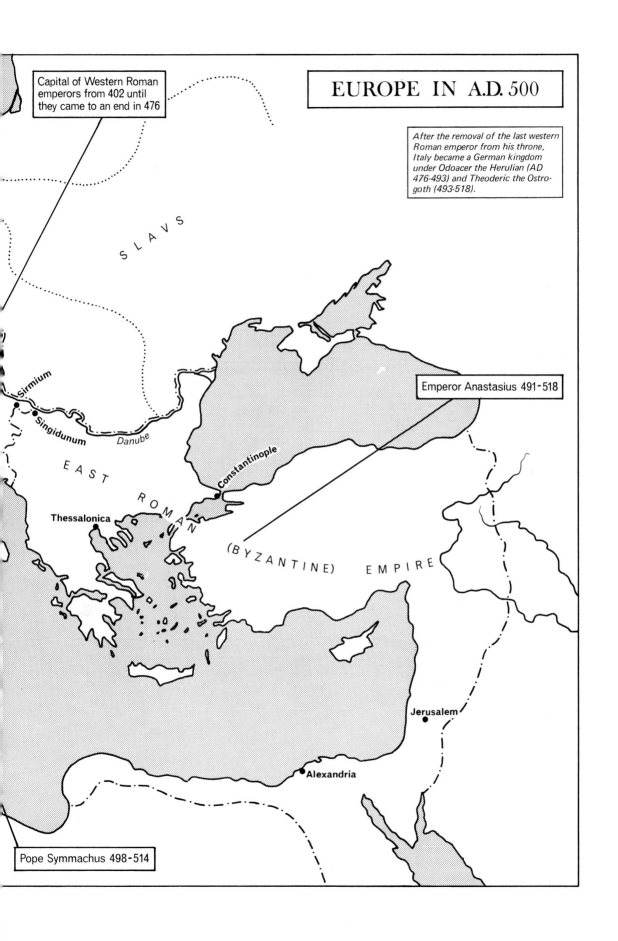

EUROPE IN A.D. 500

Capital of Western Roman emperors from 402 until they came to an end in 476

After the removal of the last western Roman emperor from his throne, Italy became a German kingdom under Odoacer the Herulian (AD 476-493) and Theoderic the Ostrogoth (493-518).

SLAVS

Sirmium

Singidunum

Danube

EAST

ROMAN

Constantinople

Thessalonica

(BYZANTINE) EMPIRE

Emperor Anastasius 491-518

Jerusalem

Alexandria

Pope Symmachus 498-514

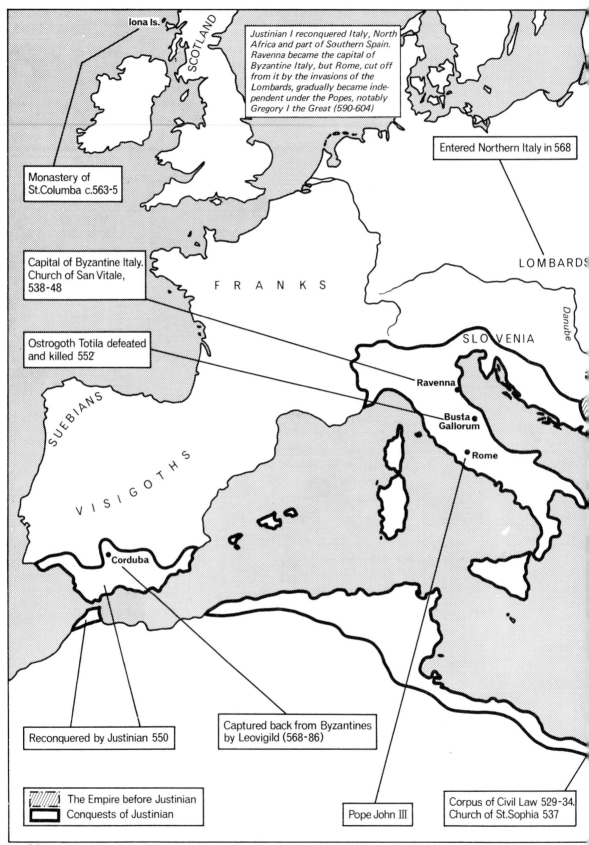

Iona Is.

SCOTLAND

Justinian I reconquered Italy, North
Africa and part of Southern Spain.
Ravenna became the capital of
Byzantine Italy, but Rome, cut off
from it by the invasions of the
Lombards, gradually became inde-
pendent under the Popes, notably
Gregory I the Great (590-604)

Entered Northern Italy in 568

Monastery of
St.Columba c.563-5

Capital of Byzantine Italy.
Church of San Vitale,
538-48

F R A N K S

LOMBARDS

Danube

Ostrogoth Totila defeated
and killed 552

SLOVENIA

Ravenna

SUEBIANS

Busta
Gallorum

Rome

V I S I G O T H S

Corduba

Reconquered by Justinian 550

Captured back from Byzantines
by Leovigild (568-86)

The Empire before Justinian
Conquests of Justinian

Pope John III

Corpus of Civil Law 529-34.
Church of St.Sophia 537

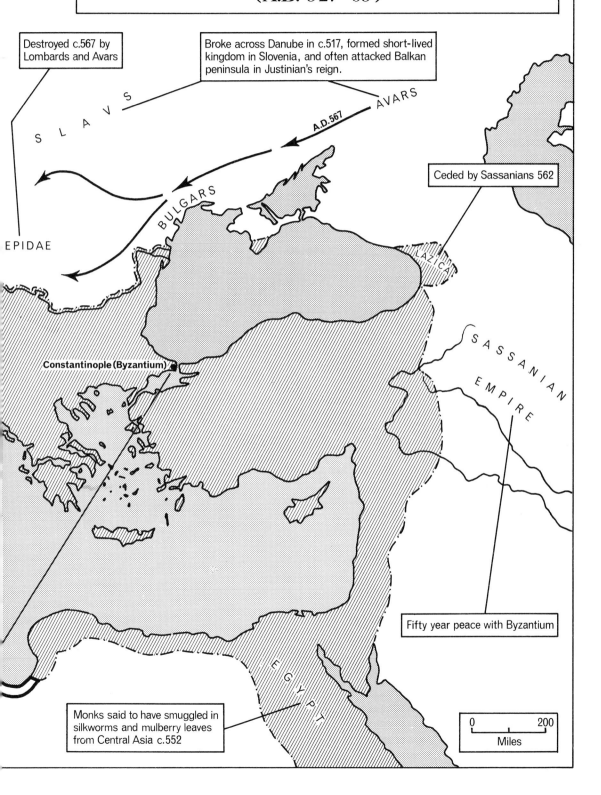

THE BYZANTINE EMPIRE OF JUSTINIAN I
(A.D. 527-65)

Destroyed c.567 by Lombards and Avars

Broke across Danube in c.517, formed short-lived kingdom in Slovenia, and often attacked Balkan peninsula in Justinian's reign.

S L A V S

AVARS

A.D. 567

BULGARS

EPIDAE

LAZICA

Ceded by Sassanians 562

SASSANIAN

EMPIRE

Constantinople (Byzantium)

Fifty year peace with Byzantium

E G Y P T

Monks said to have smuggled in silkworms and mulberry leaves from Central Asia c.552

0   200
Miles

Index of Place Names[1]

Modern names are given in brackets

---

[1] I have sometimes sacrificed consistency of spelling to convenience and tradition.